GIRL, INTERRUPTED

GIRL, INTERRUPTED

Screenplay by
James Mangold and
Lisa Loomer and
Anna Hamilton Phelan

Based on the book by
Susanna Kaysen

faber and faber

First published in 2000
by Faber and Faber Limited
3 Queen Square London WC1N 3AU
Published in the United States by Faber and Faber Inc.
a division of Farrar, Straus and Giroux Inc., New York

Photoset by Parker Typesetting Service, Leicester
Printed in England by Mackays of Chatham plc, Chatham, Kent

Screenplay based on the book 'Girl, Interrupted' by Susanna Kaysen

Special thanks Elyse Cogan, Esther Margolis, Lance Stockton
and Octavia Wiseman

A CIP record for this book is available
from the British Library

ISBN 0–571–20211–X

2 4 6 8 10 9 7 5 3 1

CONTENTS

JAMES MANGOLD SPEAKS TO TOD LIPPY

TODD LIPPY: *How did you get involved with this project?*
JAMES MANGOLD: I was in the last weeks of directing *CopLand*, and I got word through my manager that Winona had loved *Heavy* (it had just been released) and wanted to meet so we could talk about *Girl, Interrupted*. I was sent the existing screenplay but I have to admit, I didn't really connect with it. However, I set a date to meet Winona anyway – I've always thought she was a brilliant actress. There's something very 'silent movie' about Noni's acting style, a quality I really adore. It's not a 'style' in the sense of a pose or put-on, but something very organic and completely unique to her. I'm also fascinated by this fragile energy that follows her through all her films, regardless of genre.

So, despite having misgivings about the script, I met her a few days after I wrapped *CopLand*. I should also point out how flattered I was that Noni's interest in working with me was motivated solely from seeing *Heavy*. At that moment, the hoopla around *CopLand* was pretty intense. I was suddenly perceived as this guy making 'the next *Pulp Fiction*' with this mega-pop macho cast. It was a little terrifying. Most of the scripts coming to me were all cop movies, action pictures, things that people felt fitted the '*CopLand* profile'. *Heavy* had opened strongly in a few theaters in New York and Los Angeles, but a good part of the entertainment world had never seen it. And then here was Winona who had seen my fragile first movie several times and could recall scenes down to the gesture. It was touching.

Which did you read first, Susanna Kaysen's book or the script?
The producer, Cathy Konrad, and I read the script first. We were both a bit underwhelmed – it wasn't badly written, but there wasn't a clear handle on the movie yet. Then we read Susanna's book and we were more curious. The book is fascinating, mysterious, elliptical and deeply poetic. In short, a really hard nut to crack. While the existing screenplay included most of the big 'events' from the book – what few there were – I didn't feel like it captured the

book's unique tone or point of view. It's odd, because in many ways the preceding writers' scripts were much more loyal to the literal incidents of the book than mine.

So what happened when you met with Winona Ryder?
As I said, it was only days after I wrapped *CopLand*. I was exhausted. I met Winona at a hotel in New York. We both got along really well, almost immediately. But I felt badly, in a way, because no matter how much I admired her work or enjoyed Noni's company, I was hesitant to get involved with this project. I mean, I was grasping at straws in detailing how I would attack this project, and half the time I was just avoiding the topic. All I could tell her for sure was that Susanna's book had qualities that the screenplay (at that time) did not, and whatever attack someone brought to this material, it had to be bold and extreme and not just an effort to make a weepy TV movie with a lot of pretty girls in smocks.

I tried to lay out the challenges in the material, even though I didn't have any solutions. For instance, in *One Flew Over the Cuckoo's Nest*, you had a protagonist who is highly rational, playing the system, so you never face the problem you have with *Girl, Interrupted*, which is that Susanna does in fact have a problem. Whether it's adolescence, insanity or something in between is a question the movie asks. But the antagonist of this story is her mind, not cruel ward nurses. To make this story work, I felt you somehow had to dramatize the battle between the rational side of Susanna (the lucid narrator with a sharp eye) and the crazier one (the girl who was banging her wrist and flip-flopping through time and swallowing aspirins). I thought those two girls had to be seen separately, which is what, in some sense, happens in the book. The book has this tension that exists between a highly rational narrator talking about the times when she isn't sure she was rational.

Which is her unique perspective – as she mentions in the book, the irrationality of her 'episodes' is something she was always aware of, even as they were taking place.
Yeah, Susanna was always extremely lucid. But because the movie isn't the remembrance of a woman looking back (like the book), but rather, is present tense, you have to break these two Susannas

away from each other. In some way, I thought you had to make the 'illness', or whatever it was, something you could touch or see. As I explained to Winona, if you don't do that, then it could end up being a movie about an impenetrable girl who looks really sad all the time.

So my first instinct – which was bizarre and ultimately misguided – was to make the movie into a monster film, in which somehow we make this 'thing' – this blackness – palpable and real, so that you can see it. Not 'see it' like a hallucination, but make it a genuine antagonist – the thing in shadows, the thing inside death. I mean, what if death's living manifestation were insanity? What if the way the devil calls you to death is to suck the rationality out of you until the only choice remaining is a self-induced, peaceful end?

Anyway, that was the only handle I had on this material. [*Laughs.*] It was risky, and I was sure this big studio in Hollywood that owned the book (Columbia Pictures) would not respond to it. But I guess Winona liked the fact that I was taking a sledgehammer to everything, just saying, if we were to do this, we would have to do some really big thinking, and make it unlike any other movie about this topic we've seen before.

Were there other films about insanity you had in mind in that regard?
Well, there seem to be two archetypes. The first is *One Flew Over the Cuckoo's Nest*, where the protagonist is not really insane. The other type is the *Good Will Hunting, Marnie, Ordinary People* configuration, where the protagonist is battling madness, but they are surrounded with highly rational, healthy supportive characters. At the climax of this second type of story, the damaged protagonist confesses a deep secret to one of the rational supporting players – some Freudian trauma that occurred in their youth, whether it's Marnie's hooker mom beating a sailor to death, or Will Hunting's father burning him with cigarettes. And that big confession, in a sense, initiates the character's recovery, and healing.

However, one of the unique elements of Susanna's book was that she maintained that there was no deep or sordid secret in her past. I mean, when I spoke with Susanna, I grilled her. I was like, 'You're sure there's nothing?' I mean, I don't have a psychological position on whether everybody with mental problems has a secret or not, but it was clear to me that in the world of movies, they always do. This made me very interested in the question – whether you could lose your ability to function in the world without a dark secret in your past. One of the things Susanna brought up to me in those conversations was the story about her being carried across country as an infant, strapped to that board.

I assumed that was your invention, since it doesn't appear in the book.
It's something that actually happened to Susanna. In fact, I shot a little sequence of a baby strapped on a board, but it just got too goofy when I cut it in.

Anyway, after that meeting with Noni, I just hung out in New York cutting *CopLand*, talking with Cathy about it all, and slowly and quietly starting to believe that we could make *Girl, Interrupted* work. Then I came out to LA, and met with some of the executives at Columbia. I presented this whole 'monster' theory, and in truth, I think everyone thought I was totally insane, but I had gotten so amped about these ideas, I think they were just excited to have someone ready to roll up their sleeves and work on a project that had run aground.

They made a deal for Cathy and I and then I started reading and scribbling all these notes to myself about things like, you know, Winston Churchill's black dog – his depressions – and shadows on the ceiling I would stare at when I was a kid – I was trying to understand how I could weave all of these images and ideas about depression and death and childhood fear together. I watched *Repulsion* over and over. In that movie, her apartment, and the world and these people intruding on her space all become manifestations of this monster. And I watched Jack Clayton's *The Innocents*, too.

Because I was so busy cutting *CopLand* at that time, however, we hired Anna Hamilton Phelan to try out this 'monster strategy'. Anna gave it her all, but as her work came in what became immediately apparent was that this strategy was turning a very personal book into a half-baked *Exorcist*. Anna was making all kinds of great discoveries, some of which are in the final screenplay – but I realized this 'monster' idea wasn't working. The themes of the book weren't becoming any clearer, they were getting lost under the weight of this 'haunting'. It was still too much horror for this material. So when I got free of *CopLand* and Anna had to start on another film, I attacked the script myself. I felt guilty – I'd taken this movie on an eight-month journey to nowhere.

As is often the case in movies, by the time you finish your film – with all the collaborations between the studio, your producing partner, the actors, the editor – your original strategy has been watered down. But the stronger your original strategy is, the more of its boldness remains. Sometimes I think the failure of the 'monster' pass yielded a pretty good fallback position, which I don't know I would have found if I hadn't come at the material so hard initially.

Were there any other films that you had in mind at this point?
MGM'S musical of *The Wizard of Oz*, George Roy Hill's *Slaughterhouse Five*, and Michael Powell's *Black Narcissus* – the latter two utilizing a flashback structure in different ways.

When I write, I'm always looking for a template. I believe David Mamet said he likes to have a fable in mind when he's writing a screenplay – no matter how complex or contemporary the story may be, he wants a kind of guiding fable. This is very true for me – it could be Sisyphus, it could be Hansel and Gretel, but I need some kind of architecture to hang things on.

So I kept thinking, 'What is Susanna's parallel fable? What tale captures the themes of this story in a nutshell?' I tried to tell myself the story of Susanna's book at the bare-bones level – I said to myself, 'OK, it's the story of this girl, she's depressed and confused, and tortured about her home life, she feels like the world is bland and gray and full of liars and fakers, and no one gets her. She senses there must be something more, somewhere, and one day she finds herself in a cab, heading off to a strange new universe. There she meets all these amazing other young people, people also missing some parts of themselves, but people who enrich and transport her, people who become the greatest friendships of her life, and in the act of going through the struggles of living with these friends for two years, she miraculously and quietly ends up sidestepping her sadness, and landing back in the world.

And then it hit me. It's *The Wizard of Oz*! To start with, there's the obvious parallels, and then it occurred to me how incredibly Freudian the movie was – how everyone in The Wizard of Oz is missing some part of their psyche: missing courage, missing love, missing smarts. In a sense, Dorothy was also missing something – happiness. Let's face it, 'Over the Rainbow' is a song of longing and depression – not only that, but, incidentally, it's sung by a fragile young movie star who suffered from depression. And then it occurred to me, 'My God, Winona is Judy Garland,' in the sense of having this unique, fragile quality of being forever young, trapped in childhood, looking out from it, longing to climb out of it.

Also, when I watched The Wizard of Oz as a child, I was always struck by the message of Glinda the Good at the end: 'You could have gone home anytime you wanted to go home, Dorothy. All you had to do was say "There's no place like home".' That was the 'no secret' ending I was looking for! Susanna runs around chasing these different feelings, trapped in this alternate world, trying to do what's required to get out, but ultimately all that's needed for her to leave is to find within herself the commitment to leave, a renewed belief in the real world, despite its shortcomings. It seemed to me that this was the only way out of Susanna's story. It wasn't about digging deeper and deeper in analysis and finding some buried, shameful secret, but instead, it was about realizing that love is the only thing that can heal and make us grow and the friendships Susanna makes in this hospital grow her up, and prepare her for the world.

Anyway, that all hit me at once like thunder. I'd been collecting all these BFI books about the greatest films in history, and Salman Rushdie had written one of them about The Wizard of Oz. Reading it, I came upon a passage that I thought was absolutely magnificent. Rushdie said 'The Wizard of Oz is a film whose driving force is the inadequacy of adults, even of good adults, and how the weakness of grownups forces children to take control of their own destinies and so, ironically, grow up themselves.' I get chills every time I read that, because, first of all, it's a beautiful sentence. Second of all, it is a brilliant observation, and thirdly, it's a very concise concept to build a movie around.

So, I just sat down trying to figure out what more I could learn from this very unique fable. One of the first things these comparisons reinforced was my instinct to get Susanna into the hospital quickly. Even when I was eight years old, *The Wizard of Oz* took way too long to get Dorothy to Oz. By the time she was in that railroad car with Mr Magicko or whatever and the crystal ball, I was always just losing it – I wanted the tornado, I wanted Oz!

Spending most of the first act getting to know Susanna outside the hospital posed many problems the previous writers had encountered. By the time she was in the hospital, every friendship she made was handicapped by the fact that these girls were going to have to catch up with the audience. We would have already gone through all these lessons about our protagonist, and now we were going to have to sit around watching her new friends go through the same lessons. I had to get to the hospital faster, but I couldn't draw things in the comic-book fashion in which they're presented in *The Wizard of Oz*, because I had to impart a lot of serious information – Susanna's having dalliances with a friend of her father, she's disaffected from her parents and other kids, her attempted suicide, etc. All these points had to be made quickly.

Then one night I sat down and watched *Slaughterhouse Five* – not because I thought it would be relevant to my struggle, but because a new DVD had just come out. I'm a big George Roy Hill fan. *Slaughterhouse* is clearly a movie about someone who from the outside would be considered insane, a character who believes he's living in three times and places all at once. But because the movie itself uses its essential qualities – the ability to cut back and forth in time – as a tool to penetrate Billy Pilgrim's crazy existence, it somehow meant we were on the journey with him and perhaps he wasn't nuts at all. I felt like perhaps I could use this technique to get what I was always after when I was working with Anna and trying to put a mental monster in the film. Snapping forward and back again, as in *Slaughterhouse*, might make Susanna's disorientation visible, even rational.

It also makes it visceral, because the viewers are jumping back and forth with her, as opposed to hearing about her jumping back and forth. Right. I gave away oozing plates and surreal CGI moments just to use film at its most basic – the cut – to say that we can all get subverted by memory. I think that's why we connect with Billy Pilgrim – because we all have some modest version of that confusion in our lives, where we're in a conversation, and suddenly for some reason our mind goes to a terrible breakup, or a trauma with our parents or something: we go away, and then come back. To me, the goal was always to get the audience to connect with their own dysfunctional moments. If Susanna's mental troubles were only amplified versions of things we've all experienced, then we'd always cling to her as a protagonist. We'd never feel like we needed rational supporting players to help 'save' her. I wanted her to be one of the most rational characters in the film.

The most resonant part of the movie in that regard is the 'checks' scene early on, when Susanna keeps falling back to sleep in between these abrupt visits from the nurse, having flashbacks to her night with Toby months earlier. The pull of the unconscious in that kind of half-awake state is familiar to everyone.

And as we're getting to know her through these flashbacks, the other characters are getting to know her, too. So then later, like in the scene in the ice-cream shop where Lisa says 'Is this the professor's wife?', we understand that, even though we've never seen them have a conversation about it, that element of her life is something she has certainly talked to them about. What got me even more excited about this technique was trying to stage these transitions very aggressively so that the two scenes were always graphically similar. One of my favourite cuts occurs during that scene you mentioned in the hospital, with Winona, her head on the pillow, looking to – *cut* – her naked boyfriend on the other side of the bed, staring back at her from his pillow. We tried to do those graphical matches in every transition. You know, Winona walking out the door of her boyfriend's apartment and finding a nurse, who then is saying 'Checks'. Not to be clever, or athletic, but to try to emulate the way we can slip in and out of memory, instead of doing the kind of clichéd, warbly dissolve into the past and then warbly dissolve back to the present.

The scene that got me in *Slaughterhouse Five* was the very fiirst scene in which you have Billy sitting at his typewriter, writing, 'I move back and forth in time.' He suddenly hears a loud engine, looks up, and he's in a snowy woods. And all I could think was that if somewhere in the first five minutes of *Girl*, if I could utilize that technique, and get away with it, I'd have a protagonist who had a simple problem – they're lost in a loop of their life.

But as with Slaughterhouse, I didn't want every one of these 'time jumps' to be enormously 'significant' in and of themselves. Meaning, the flashback scenes weren't necessarily violent breakups or someone asking you to marry them – they were each just a piece of a puzzle. The sum of these pieces would be a knowledge of this girl.

Which is very true to the spirit of the book, which consists of short, almost fragmentary chapters consisting of little glimpses into her various experiences.

It is very true in Susanna's book. The whole is greater than the sum of its parts. Also, I was trying to avoid a kind of Screenplay 101, which would be just hitting all these clear bullet points of backstory, and then sending her into the institution. I lose interest so quickly if I sense those kinds of structures. I just get bored trying to write them – no amount of cigarettes or caffeine can make my fingers move on the keyboard – I feel like I'm making something I've already seen. When I'm pleased with myself, it's always because I'm making something I haven't seen before.

It's not like I consider myself Mr Avant-garde; I'm fascinated by well-done straight-ahead movies. But it bores me to go from plot point to plot point, being able to predict everything that's coming. I mean, part of drama is sensing what's coming, but at the same time things should seem shockingly unpredictable. Alexander MacKendrick always had this great expression, that what happens at the end of a movie should be the only thing that ever could have happened, but yet it must feel completely unanticipated. In retrospect it has to seem the only way things could have gone, yet unexpected. That's a very difficult trick to pull off.

How did Black Narcissus *influence the writing of the film?*
That was banging around in my head because it's about five women in a very circumscribed, magical universe – another kind of a vacuum, a convent – fighting against their demons. What really influenced me from *Black Narcissus* was the ending, when one nun goes quite mad, putting on the lipstick and red dress, running around and trying to kill Deborah Kerr. I wanted the same kind of strong, ballsy ending for *Girl, Interrupted*. Despite the

fact that this was a bit of a leap from what actually happened in the book, it felt like the only way dramatically to realize Susanna's struggle with madness and her resultant commitment to live in the world was to have a final showdown between her and a character strongly representing the exhilarating freedom of insanity. Susanna, in essence, is torn between being another grownup zombie in the real world, with all the sadnesses and compromises that entails, or giving herself up to this other kind of zombiehood that Lisa represents.

Also, that scene also calls up the struggle between the id *and the ego, taking place as it does in the dark depths of the hospital's tunnels –*
Yeah, I thought about that. Also in Oz at the Witch's castle. It was also really clear to me, even if it never happened, that there was a kind of – I mean, I said this to Susanna Kaysen – it seemed to me she had fallen in love with Lisa. And if this movie had any form, it seemed it had to be as a love story that ended with a breakup. They may get together later, run into each other, but that breakup had to somehow be tied to Susanna's recovery.

How did Susanna Kaysen respond to that, or, for that matter, the dramatic structure you came up with for the film?
When she read the screenplay, she was – well, I don't want to put words in her mouth, but I was incredibly relieved with the enthusiasm she showed for what I'd done. And as for the places where I departed from the facts as she presented them, she'd be the first to say she combined characters and made simplifications and changes to reality to make her book work. So I think the dramatic conflagration at the end wasn't disturbing to her, because she thought of Susanna in the movie as a different Susanna from her. I think that's the only healthy way to approach these things. She created a fable out of her own life, and I was creating a movie out of her fable. So I had the distance to understand. Her biggest reaction was that I really got the character of Lisa.

That's interesting, because so much of Lisa's dialogue is yours.
It was the same kind of space I went into when I wrote Ray Liotta's role in *CopLand*. It was the same voice in me. Lisa was a very freeing character to write – as it was for Angie to play.

I remember in one of our earlier interviews you talked about how, despite your love for wordless characters, you have a side that loves to 'go on rants'. Was that something you were accessing when you were writing Lisa's character?

I enjoyed speaking through her. One day as I was driving, I came up with this line of dialogue. I raced into the office and wrote it down on a blank piece of paper and called my assistant Lance in, and read it. 'A man is a dick is a man is a dick is a chicken is a dad, a valium, a speculum, a cucumber . . . ' I had been struggling with that Daisy scene – I had needed a culmination, not merely of the drama, but a culmination of Lisa's poetry. It had to be a startling and rhythmically interesting line that also stung. Lance and I were like, 'Wow, that's intense.' I was sure the studio was going to cut it. Anyway, I just went back and built the scene toward that statement.

I've never come at a movie less structurally and more from the gut. For instance, I wrote the first two pages – that silent movie of shots in the tunnels – and all I knew at the time I wrote it was that I had to have a conflagration at the end, so I decided that's how I would make myself write it. I would describe the aftermath of the scene, and then I'd just have to write my way up to that aftermath. I had no idea how I was going to get there – to this room with a burning furnace and a rattling window and broken glass and a cat – I just laid it down for myself as a dare. That was also inspired by *Slaughterhouse Five* – the idea that the first thing we see is one of the last scenes in the narrative. And then we flash backward, and then flash back further from there, swirling around until we find the present tense of the movie, all the time marching toward that climax in the furnace room.

I also felt like I had to promise the audience something intense if they were going to live through this meditative, flip-floppy first act. They had to know they were heading to a charged dramatic place.

Could you talk about how your knowing that Winona Ryder would be playing Susanna from the beginning affected the writing of Susanna's character?

Not only was the world of Susanna Kaysen and those realities merging with my own voice and experiences, but the intricacies of

Noni's personality were feeding the writing. I found I was drawing from both women, making a 'hybrid' Susanna. Some of the experiences Winona has had growing up, many of them in the strange fishbowl of stardom – these experiences were not dissimilar to the strange 'through the looking-glass' journey of Susanna Kaysen. Like I said before, I'm less interested in affected performances, where someone becomes someone else. What's always inspiring to me is when an actor puts themselves onscreen. Winona understood the kind of openness I was expecting from her and she expected the same of herself. Exposing your soul to a lens six inches from your nose can be a lot more difficult than 'putting on' a character, developing a limp and an strange accent.

We've discussed how aggressive this adaptation is in many regards, owing to the fact that you've added to and modified the original source material pretty dramatically, but I was interested to find so many small details in the book, even when taken out of context, plugged back into the film. There are too many to mention, but I'll give you one example: you give Georgina a line of dialogue in the film about her dad being in the CIA that her boyfriend, Wade, had in the book.

Well, when I was writing *Heavy* and *CopLand*, I had all these memories of growing up in the Hudson Valley – experiences, sights, faces, memories I could touch and taste and smell – and they anchored me as I wrote the fictionalized worlds of those movies. With *Girl, Interrupted*, I clearly had to make some kind of adjustment – so I tried to absorb Susanna Kaysen's book, and, in a sense, make it my memory. As I wrote, I drew upon Susanna's memories – as I had drawn upon my own while writing *CopLand* or *Heavy*. Even with the first two films, nothing was ever quite the same as it made its translation to screen, but it was my anchor.

Susanna's book wasn't just a narrative, but a world of detail and impression and feeling. By the second draft, I was also having dialogues with Susanna directly – I would grab at her life and her way of looking at things for solutions to dramatic problems, twisting these pieces of reality like a pretzel – not to distort them, but in order to try and find a way to make a truer film. The book contains a tremendous amount of detail. There were so many details, like her French cigarettes, or her fixation with her hand – things that led me places.

Also, I tried to try to weave a sense of destiny into the film – to suggest that maybe Susanna's 'madness' was a kind of prescience about where she might be headed, or the challenges she was going to face. For instance, perhaps her obsessing over the bones in her hand was a vague 'knowing' that someday she was going to slam a door on her hand. None of these ideas plays in an overt way, but to me, weaving these pieces, giving them an amplified *Oz*-like significance, was an interesting way to further ask the questions Susanna was asking – as opposed to maintaining a literal, cut-and-dried loyalty to the book, I was trying to be loyal to the ideas in the book and perhaps amplify and renew them.

Many character details in the book have been broadened considerably, or in some cases, completely changed. In the book, Polly, for instance, had a much less compelling story about why she burned herself than the one Georgina relates in the film about her losing her puppy.
Much of that comes from the *Wizard of Oz* template, that every character needed a greater kind of mythology than Susanna provided, like the Tin Man's 'I've been sitting here rusting ever since . . . ' In fact, in the early drafts, I used Susanna's backstory about Polly – that she set herself on fire with a book of matches for no apparent reason – but as the script began to take on a life of its own, it felt like that ambiguity belonged to Susanna. If every character had an ambiguous backstory it would defeat Susanna's point instead of furthering it. When Susanna was writing the book, she established in every girl a kind of mystery about what had struck them. But as I was writing the movie, it felt like that point was getting overstressed. It seemed to me that the mystery of Susanna's illness would gain intensity if many of the girls around her had very good reasons for being at the hospital. Then Susanna would be a unique character – not unlike Dorothy – someone who found herself in a mythological world, but who herself possessed no mythology, no secret.

Even Lisa reveals a secret at the end, mentioning that her parents think she's a whore and wish she were dead. And of course Daisy reveals the incestuous relationship with her father. Georgina reveals Polly's story, but of course you don't even know whether to believe it or not. I always thought that was one of the weirdest, most twisted parts of the movie. One of my biggest notes to Clea

Duvall, who played Georgina, was to really enjoy the telling of Polly's tale. To relish the magic of telling Susanna a story late at night – that this magic far exceeded the sombre tragedy of Polly's past. Not because Georgina was insensitive, but because part of the charm of this hospital was that everyone's personal tragedies were kind of irrelevent.

What happened to Georgina's boyfriend, Wade, who's another patient in the hospital in the book?
He was in some of the other writers' drafts, but it didn't really lead anywhere. It's not that the scenes were badly written; I just felt that if I were going to invest time in Georgina, I wanted to give her a more magical identity than that. There was something flat about it.

Also, in the book it seems to be there for Susanna's internal voice to muse about not wanting a 'crazy' – i.e. a fellow patient – boyfriend.
To me, if Susanna and Lisa were the most sexually aware young women on the ward, it offered a kind of clarity about why they become close. It followed then that everyone else had to be a kind of child. From the moment I started writing, I felt there needed to be an order in this universe; and this made Lisa's attraction to Susanna logical – she found a friend who's also been living in the world, who wasn't stuck in childhood. In order to make this clear, I steered away from overt sexuality among the supporting characters.

I was a little nervous, however, that on the page Polly and Georgina would be too similar. But as we were rehearsing, I saw that they could be played quite differently. Clea was to be more of a granola type, more sexually aware and more folky, listening to Joni Mitchell, whereas Polly was still playing with plastic horses, which is something I took from Cathy Konrad's childhood. Cathy still knows the names of all these beautifully painted plastic horses from the sixties that she used to collect. Also, an old friend of mine, Lisa Krueger, made a brilliant short film about a girl who had this sweet pre-pubescent horse-love. So Polly became that girl – an innocent who always wanted to play musical instruments, who loved horses and animals. It's crazy how all of this transpires. I mean, my wife's talking to me about her childhood, and these horses, and meanwhile I'm working on the Daisy apartment scene and I've given her this cat, and then the cat comes back to the hospital. And suddenly I'm realizing, 'Oh, that could be beautiful,' because suddenly Susanna can bestow this gift on Polly as she's leaving, and fulfilling this dream – fulfilling a need of Polly's to have someone to love.

In the book, Dr Wick is described as a 'disguised boarding-school matron' who blushes every time sex is mentioned by one of the girls. Can you describe how you came to give her a much more central – and sympathetic – role in Susanna's recovery in the film?
I felt like I couldn't make every shrink an incompetent. Susanna likes to say that the events from that period in her life are a kind of 'calcified memory'. My concern was that Susanna was looking at her experiences at the hospital and was describing these doctors – who all seemed slightly boobish in the book – through the eyes of a young girl who was resistant to getting better because she was questioning the existence of an illness. But someone there had to be effective. I mean, the hospital Susanna is referring to in the book was a very respected place, located at the heart of American academia. A lot of famous people – Sylvia Plath, Ray Charles, James Taylor – went there, and I guess I just couldn't believe that they would've stayed there if they were encountering nothing but idiots.

Also, it would be a sad cliché if every shrink scene featured an ineffectual psychologist. I didn't want Melvin to be an idiot, either; I wanted him to be a kind of workaday shrink with a lot of difficult patients. But for Dr Wick, I needed someone of grandeur and weight to come into the movie, to get to the heart of the matter with Susanna, but someone who does it so effectively that it's almost too much for Susanna to bear. I needed someone to cut to the quick, and lay out for Susanna and the audience exactly what Susanna was going to have to do to get out of there. You know, 'This has all been a bit fun, but let's cut the shit.' I kept thinking of characters like Hannibal Lecter, with that ability to pierce a hero's psyche. Or even James Mason in *The Verdict*.

The surprising thing was that Vanessa brought such warmth to the role. We rehearsed it at first, trying the scene with a more aggressive tone, but the beauty of Vanessa's performance was to watch her methodically, and rather kindly, unravel Susanna.

Anyway, the short answer is that the movie really couldn't operate if Dr Crumble was a jerk, if Melvin was less than effectual, and then Dr Wick turned out to be a schoolmarm boob. The movie would have become less rich, and more one-dimensional. I also thought this was one place where we could be very different from *One Flew Over the Cuckoo's Nest*.

Can you talk a little bit about the writing of that scene between Susanna and Dr Wick?

A couple of years ago, Winona was hanging out in my office, right after she'd wrapped *Alien Resurrection*, and I was sharing with her some of what I was doing to the script and some of the questions facing me. I tossed these questions to Noni and she wasn't taking a strong position. It shocked me a little, her hesitance to stake out a position unless she was absolutely sure – it's certainly a rare quality in show business. And so I said, 'You're a really ambivalent person, aren't you?' and she looked up kind of curiously.

Anyway, when she left, I opened my dictionary and looked up the word 'ambivalent'. I've used the word all my life, and always thought it meant 'I don't care', or 'I don't know', or 'I don't have an investment either way'. But according to the dictionary the word actually describes someone with a monstrous investment in two opposing courses of action. I suddenly realized my first two movies were all about ambivalence – how someone can be seduced by both sides of a conflict.

So I started playing with the word 'ambivalence' in the dialogue of the Dr Wick scene, and I realized that I could take advantage of the fact that many of us misunderstand the meaning of the word. So after Dr Wick tells Susanna that her progress has plateaued, and asks if that disappoints her, Susanna very curtly replies, 'I'm ambivalent. In fact, that's my new favorite word.' At that point I wanted Susanna to appear to get the better of Dr Wick for a moment. Even if Wick was the smartest shrink in the world, I wanted the scene to have a flow to it. So when Wick asks Susanna if she knows what the word means, Susanna responds, 'I don't care.' Wick replies 'Well, if it's your favorite word I would've thought that you – ' And Susanna snaps, 'It means "I don't care".' It's like Susanna got the better of her but then of course

Vanessa gets back on top. It's one of my favourite scenes in the movie. I love that whole interplay, and thought it somehow got to the heart of the movie. I also love the stillness of that scene.

What about the scene in which Susanna and Lisa escape from the hospital and visit Daisy? How did that evolve?
The runaway to Daisy's had a very peculiar evolution. I kept getting hit by how undramatic it was to have this scene play as it does in the book, in which they get a postcard and Valerie gathers the ward together to announce Daisy's suicide. First of all, even if it happened that way, it was hard to believe. Gathering all these troubled girls together and announcing that their friend has killed herself – it seemed highly unproductive. I didn't know how to resolve Daisy. I remember saying to Anna Hamilton Phelan as she was writing, 'If Daisy dies, then we're going to have to see it.' I had this idea that when Lisa ran away, you could crosscut between her and Susanna, and you could see that Lisa seeks out Daisy and 'undoes' her.

It was Cathy who suggested, 'Just let them both out of the hospital. Let them run away together and go to Daisy's.' I guess I had been a little trapped by my fear of breaking from the book. It was Cathy who gave me the courage to say, 'I need an event here, and it ain't in the book.' So suddenly things just started to line up. If you have this character, Susanna, whose disease is enigmatic – if it even exists at all – then what is the logical way for her to behave? The closer someone gets to pinning her down, the more she's going to want to get out. Also, if Lisa represents the beauty of a creature ruled by passion and not reason, then it seemed logical that at a certain point in Susanna's trajectory, she'd run away with madness. That became the physical act of running away, and running from the people who were on to her game. So this became an opportunity to write what I thought could be an eerie set piece in which Lisa reveals her contempt for normalcy, even the fucked-up 'normalcy' of Daisy's situation, and where she could ruthlessly pull the veil off of it – forcing Susanna to confront the downside of Lisa's inhibitions.

I also felt there was a good parallel between the way Wick pressed so hard on Susanna and Lisa pressed so hard on Daisy. If you thought Wick was applying pressure to Susanna, Lisa was off the charts – brutal and unflinching and cruel. I wanted it to be a really conflicting scene for the audience, where everything she's saying seems entirely true but terribly wrong at the same time.

The other thing that scene provided me with was a chance to stage the standard intervention scene – the revelation of the buried 'secret' – with someone other than my protagonist. I felt that if I could deliver a revelatory scene about a repressed psychological secret to the audience, then I might be freed from having to do it again with Susanna. And more obviously, it was a chance for Susanna to see what the 'dark side' of Lisa's freedom could yield.

How about the ice-cream parlor scene? In the book, Kaysen describes this as a fairly common ritual for the girls.
Well, again, every scene has to have a greater role in the movie. It can't just be there for its texture. In Susanna's book, there were these wonderful snapshots of tension as the nurses escorted the girls down the street. Anyway, I needed something to happen in the scene besides the girls just misbehaving, which is basically all that happens in the book. I think it was while I was working with Anna that it occurred to us that we could put Mrs Gilcrest at another table in the scene – in the background, basically. But it wasn't until much later, when the studio was pressuring me to cut the scene, that I realized how to make something even more out of it. The idea came to me when we cast Mary Kay Place in the role. Cathy had known Mary Kay through *Citizen Ruth*.

When she accepted the role, it really galvanized me to make this scene worthy of such a wonderful actress. And suddenly it was so obvious! Susanna's been screwing Mrs. Gilcrest's husband – it's a dramatic necessity that she come at this girl, directly, in a full-on attack. And it's so perfect in the timing of the story because it's a chance then for Lisa to show Susanna what a good thing it is to have a friend with big balls.

It's also a great way to illustrate Susanna finally – and joyously – surrendering herself to this new universe. Finally giving up her resistance to being 'one of – '
'Them'. Right. They now become her family. When something hostile and disapproving comes at her, and she doesn't know what to say, this new world of loyalties comes to her defense. What I did draw from Susanna's book was that after you've hung out in a

place like Claymoore for a while and made profound friendships with 'crazy' people, the normal world can start to look pretty nuts.

In the book, there's a mention of Susanna getting together with Georgina several times, and bumping into Lisa, with her child, on the street in Boston years later.

All the way to the very end, I think the studio was hoping I'd relent and do something like that. Not to knock them, but I always felt it would be like that movie that Bob De Niro made with Meryl Streep, *Falling in Love*, where they run into each other at a bookstore. To me, the romance of the film was that it was like a war movie, and the beauty of war movies is that people go through a harrowing life-changing journey together, and then have to separate and say goodbye. There's something romantic about that to me.

Like CopLand, *this film elicited an avalanche of actors' interest during the casting process. I remember there was a 'buzz' about actresses interested in playing the role of Lisa, particularly.*

I don't know what to say about the buzz thing. I knew, certainly, that Lisa on the page was a phenomenal role. I mean, Winona knew it was a phenomenal role, and there were nothing but phenomenal actresses interested in playing it.

When Angelina Jolie came in to read for Lisa, it was an amazing moment. She read not just one scene, not two scenes, but every scene Lisa had in the entire motion picture, then gave me a hug and walked out. She literally knocked the wind out of me. After that reading, there was no question. When I sent her tape to the studio, there was no question among the executives, either, even though no one had seen *Gia* yet. She was so powerful. Terrifying and charming and sexy and truthful and real. Brilliant. I mean, all of these gestures I'd written came to life without pose, without posturing. She's incredible with language, and she got the rhythms of all the verbal dances I was doing like a jazz musician. I thought, 'Man, she is going to make me look like I can write.' The press started making stuff of the 'race' for the Lisa role. In fact, after Angie read, it was pretty much over. Then Brittany read for the role of Daisy and really aced it.

Could you describe the audition process a little bit?
I don't like to call them 'auditions', because I'm embarrassed by
the kind of hiring quality of the whole event. I try to destigmatize
it as much as possible. Whenever I do a reading with an actor –
especially an actor I'm very, very interested in – I will take a lot of
time. To a point of where it's been an hour or so of really working
on the role.

I think it's totally unfair to ask an actor to come with a particular
tactic and find out whether or not it's a score. I hate the idea that
they've been home, talking with a boyfriend or an acting coach,
torturing themselves about how they're going to interpret the
material – it's such a fuckup, and it's so hurtful, and everything
comes down to this moment of whether they've guessed right. I
want them to come in neutral, and take the time with me where I
try to find a part of them that connects with some part of the role.

So you'll actually read with the actors?
Oh, yeah. On *CopLand*, I did all the reading with actors. I just like
to do it, and in that case it made sense because all the roles were
male. Lisa Beech, the casting director, did some of the reading for
Girl, Interrupted, because so many of these roles are female. She
was phenomenal, and kind of wacky, like me, in the sense that she
loves going there, getting there. One actress spat in Lisa's face
during a reading – it was crazy.

I know that some of the actors of great note who came in to read
had great times working on it, whether they got it or not, and that
was very meaningful to me, not to sound like a sap. But I hate the
hiring-or-not quality to these things; I think it's much more about
making sure that the actor is going to be brilliant in the role. It's
not about giving someone a chance, it's about going through a
process where you sense a certain potential. Otherwise, it's so
painful having the wrong person in a role.

How did you get Vanessa Redgrave?
She was the one actor I never got to meet, because she was in
London. I just made the leap because I was so crazy about her. It
was an amazing honour to have her on the film, and I think she
had a great deal of fun even though she was with us only for a
week. It was so magical the day she arrived, because she
immediately began telling me about the backstory she imagined

for Dr Wick. She had this idea that Wick's parents had been killed in World War II, and she was a Jew, and had moved or fled as a young child to South Africa, and had grown up with a relative there. And after she completed her studies, she emigrated alone to this country, where she quickly rose to prominence.

Did the other actors devise backstories for their characters as well?
Everyone had a story they were drawing upon. Angie, for instance, developed this amazingly rich backstory about how she accidentally killed her baby brother or sister – I can't remember which it was – when she was young. Whoopi Goldberg was drawing upon her mother, who was a nurse at, I believe, New York Hospital. In many ways, this for her was a real tribute to her mother, whom she really admired for having great dignity, yet also having the ability to keep a certain distance. You know, the fine balance someone has to employ in doing a job like that between feeling too much and feeling too little.

How did Whoopi Goldberg become involved with the film?
Whoopi was tracking this movie very early on, and to be honest, I was very resistant to the idea. First of all, she's a very big movie star, and I knew we couldn't afford her. You'd think because we were making a studio picture, it would be, like, 'Oh, you have more money now.' But the funny thing is because it's a big studio, actors won't work for nothing like they will on a Miramax film. Even if Miramax is owned by Disney, it doesn't matter – agents will make deals with their clients for less.

Also, I had this prejudice – she was on *Hollywood Squares*, she makes all these comedies, I'm making a big serious movie – basically, I was being a little snobbish. To her credit, though, Whoopi called my assistant, Lance, one day. I was in the office, in a panic: 'What do I do? What am I supposed to say?' This is when it's so great to have a partner who understands producing so well. So I call Cathy on another line as Whoopi's talking to Lance. 'Whoopi Goldberg's on the phone, what am I supposed to say?!' Cathy was really into the idea, but I was much more suspect about what it was going to say about the movie, and what kind of job she was going to do. So Whoopi says to Lance – in my first introduction to how charming she is – 'Take this down. My name is Whoopi Goldberg, and I'm very interested in playing Valerie.

I'm really a very nice person, and I would listen to everything you said, and I would work very hard on your movie.' And I think she added something like 'I don't smell, and I don't throw temper tantrums' – something very funny like that. And she was like, 'You have all that, Lance?' [*Laughs*.] And she gave him her home phone number, and said, 'Tell him to call me.'

So I called her, and told her I didn't think I could afford her, and I kind of stumbled through how I feel like I really have to get to know everybody I work with, and that I can't make a decision, even though she's a big movie star blah blah blah; how everyone – even Winona, who I got to know very well over this period of writing the script and deciding whether or not I was going to make the movie – has to go through this process so we both know we want to work together. She said, 'So come on down; I'm taping *Hollywood Squares* on Friday.'

So here I am, walking into game-show world. I go into her dressing-room, and meet her mom, and her grandkids and daughter marching in and out, and sense this tremendous amount of love and seriousness in her. But I even needed more. I went and saw her at her house, and we worked on a scene together – I don't know when anyone has put Whoopi through this, ever. Certainly not in the last ten years. I told her I needed somebody who's going to be part of an ensemble, and what that translates to when you're a movie star is that you've gotta be around when sometimes you're out of focus in the background. I remember saying to Sly, 'Some days I'm going to be shooting someone else and you're going to be sitting at a barstool in the background, and I need you there. I don't want to shoot around you; I don't want to shoot you out. I don't want to put you in a place where I can get you done with one shot and send you home. I want you to be part of the fabric of the film, even if some days you feel like you came in to do extra work.' So I got a chance – since all of life is a rehearsal, and I had already been through this once with Sly – to kind of put down these fears I had. And Whoopi said, 'I hear you. Don't worry about it.'

I quickly realized she is one hundred per cent gold. There is such dignity to her and the world she has built around herself. She is an amazingly grounded human being. She's loyal and kind to the people who work with her. She's always there on time, always working hard. She's just profoundly connected to people. I was really wrong – I'd created all these artistic boundaries about what you can and can't be, and do, and she just doesn't recognize them.

In the book, Valerie is actually white – did you write that character as black in your script?
No, that came from an early draft written by Lisa Loomer, and I just thought it was a really smart move, because in many ways, the all-whiteness of the movie did not reflect the sixties. Also, as much as I wanted to avoid shrinks that were all boobs, I wanted to avoid nurses that were all Nurse Ratcheds. And I had this idea, just in my head when I was writing – between *Jackie Brown* and all those other movies getting rereleased through Quentin's new label – about someone in a bigass Afro, with shades. When I was growing up, there was a Jamaican nurse, a friend of my family, who had this great Afro and wore shades and just looked so cool.

By the way, Whoopi was a great help to me in that she has such a maternal presence and power, even when she's not working. She really aided me in my ability to control the set, and let's face it, I had a lot of young women – and I'm not saying it's about any of them being brats, because they weren't – but they were all very young and full of life and bounce and ideas, and it could be overwhelming. There was a quality of Valerie to Whoopi, and it bled into her influence on the set itself. Everything stayed calm; things got sorted out, and went in an order. No one was going to tangle with Valerie, and no one was going to tangle with Whoopi. For instance, when Angie was playing scenes out, she was so powerful – before Whoopi arrived on the set, I'd be like, 'Oh, man, Angie is so powerful, how is Whoopi going to stop her? She doesn't fear anything.' And one of the first scenes we did was where Valerie stops Lisa from plunging the pen into her neck – and all Angie had to do was lock eyes with Whoopi to know, 'OK, I'm not fucking with you.' And I never had to worry about it.

Along those lines, did you find that the actors' relationships with one another mirrored their characters' relationships in the movie?
It's not the relationships in the movie, but everyone dug very deep into their characters. Angie was very free. I mean, there's a great deal of her that is Lisa. She's an incredible truth-teller, has a very hard time containing what she thinks, is full of ideas, insatiably

rebellious yet incredibly driven by her craft. Everyone was investigating their characters. More than everyone was their characters, everyone was going deeper and deeper into these places. The first rehearsal day, the ward wasn't fully dressed, but it was painted and the tile was down, and I got the beds in everyone's room. We had this whole floor with two hallways, and this great TV room, and I got the entire cast and the nurses in, and I just let the ward exist. I showed everyone their rooms, gave them their central props – you know, showed Polly where the horses and musical instruments were kept – and J. P., our prop guy, showed the nurses how to do beds. I just let them be, in this kind of giant organic improv.

Sometimes this kind of thing is more important than hashing out the blocking of a specific scene way in advance; I wanted to understand the blocking of the ward. How would people move around? Where would they hang out? For instance, the great scene of Winona in front of that big round window? That came from a certain point during this hour and a half, while Cynthia was fixing the TV, and Angie was sliding around the ward in a rolling chair. I discovered Winona in that vinyl couch by that window, with her legs pulled up to her chest, smoking a cigarette and watching the light through the trees. I looked at her and said, 'I don't have a single fucking scene that sees this, and I have to find one.' And when we shot that scene, it was completely improv. I had a day when I finished early, and Jack Green and I set up a camera that kind of captured the symmetry of these two benches and Winona sat down and I just said, 'All right, get up, move to here. Move to there.' We just did it in an hour, and it was all because of that one moment in rehearsal.

A lot of the little moments of that swirling montage sequence – little beats, almost *New Yorker* cartoons – came from that hour and a half – like Whoopi on a smoke break on a fire escape. That fire escape was what we called our 'deck of shame'. It's where we all went out to smoke, because the ward was too claustrophobic. Whoopi and I, or Winona and Angie, or whoever, would gather on these really cold days to smoke on the deck of shame. So on Whoopi's last day I did this shot of her looking wistfully out on the grounds as we swirled around with the camera on the deck of shame. That's the other wonderful thing about being on one location for so long – you get to know it so well, discover all the nooks and crannies.

There are a few things in the script published here that I assume were shot, and later cut in the editing process. In the screenplay, for instance, one of Lisa's first lines to Susanna is a rather odd, violent snippet of dialogue: 'I will kill you, Geisha girl.' What happened to that?
Well, this is where it gets really funny for me. As I've discussed, there's this way that, as you're writing, your character merges with your actress. I wanted to set Angie and Winona and Lisa and Susanna off in opposition at the beginning, so that line just came from how I thought Lisa would view this perfect, fragile creation. The other thing is that with this scene, I wasn't just thinking about *The Wizard of Oz*; I was using it. That scene of Lisa's arrival is the arrival of the Wicked Witch of the West. Like Dorothy, Susanna shows up and lands in the bed of a girl who, in a less obvious way, is dead because of her arrival. And Lisa arrives and realizes her friend has been replaced by this other girl.

John Gardner wrote a great book called *On Becoming a Novelist*, which has this passage where he talks about writing an entire section of a Faulkner book down just to internalize his language. When you're searching for structures, you can just steal one. Hurl your characters into these existing structures, and you'll end up throwing away most of it because the life in your characters will obliterate it anyway. That 'I'm going to kill you, Geisha girl' was a sort of 'I'll get you, my pretty, and your little dog, too'. To Angie's credit, she got what I was trying to do – I levelled about it with her – but she had a hard time saying 'I will kill you'. She came up with the line in the picture, which I think is really good: 'You're all such weak people.' It's this whole other statement about fragility and fear of the truth.

How about the scene where the girls, after sneaking into Dr Wick's office, end up having to hide from a security guard?
It was another one of these go-back-in-time moments where we flip back to a sex scene between Susanna and Professor Gilchrest. That scene was all shot, it's just one of those instances where a movie starts to speak to you. One of the things it was saying to Kevin and me in the cutting room was, 'Hey, man, this movie's about all these girls and this wonderful journey they're on

together; you can't dump them all and go into one girl's head any more.' That whole reel started becoming this passage about this band of girls befriending one another. As I started getting rid of the stuff in between, it became much more powerful; it's one of my favourite passes of the movie. You know, when you're at a screening for an audience you get to a point in the film where you can suddenly go, 'OK, I'm safe now.' And I feel that way about that whole reel – it goes from the films to the ice-cream to the montage, from the montage to Tobias arriving, to him leaving without her, to the scene with Susanna and John changing the light bulb, to the singing to Polly through the door to that scene with Dr Wick, and right to the runaway. It's a powerful segment of the movie, and what it speaks about is friendship. And anything tangential to that seemed to just fuck up this beautiful music.

Poor Winona, though. She had to do this whole thing where she's grinding up against Professor Gilchrest, palms to the wall, staring at this map of Florida hanging in front of her. [*Laughs.*] She was like, 'I can't believe you put me through that and you aren't using it.'

That light-bulb-changing scene you mentioned was my favourite in the film. Winona Ryder's performance is very moving, and it's just a wonderfully subtle moment between her and the actor who plays John. Travis Fine. I love him in the doorway, silhouetted, like it's *The Searchers*. When I was writing this movie I entered this space that was similar to the one I was in when I was writing *Heavy*. There were moments in which I wrote scenes where the exchanges were really simple, and I'm so thankful that the studio didn't encourage me to go back and overwrite them. I'm very proud of that scene – it was like a chance to put a little piece of the old me in this 'Hollywood' movie.

What's funny is how these things sometimes come to you backwards. I needed a night scene because I wanted this to go right before the Polly scene, so I was trying to figure out what John would be doing in the room at night. So I thought he could be changing a light bulb, but then I was like, 'Why would he be doing that at night?' But then I realized that's what was beautiful and odd about it. That she's sleeping, and he snuck in her room just to put in a new light bulb.

So much of the book consists of Susanna Kaysen's ruminations on madness and sanity, like her chapter on 'viscosity' versus 'velocity'.
But in a movie, can you imagine Winona sitting there talking about viscosity versus velocity? It's like, 'What's going on?' It's impenetrable. The true, loyal translation of that kind of thought into a motion picture is shooting Winona's eyes watching the world work. That was a discovery I made while making the film. The way all of that translated into the poetry of cinema was through actual cinema, not through repeating those words. I mean, I still feel slightly cheated that some of that stuff is not in the movie in a more obvious way. But then I really feel vindicated when I see that it's in the movie in a poetic way. When I hear people talk about the movie, it's so clear they've absorbed the central questions of the book.

One could say that Girl, Interrupted *is your first 'studio' film –*
I don't think that's true, but go ahead.

You would call CopLand *a studio film?*
Yes, let's be honest. I mean, the budget level is not all that different between the two movies.

But what about the whole issue of previews, test screenings, that kind of thing?
That was an issue on *CopLand*, too. Although, because this picture is so filled with comedy and love, the process was easier here simply because the previews were easier. Despite the movie's dark setting, it had so much emotion in it, and such a clear sense of change for the protagonist, that we did extremely well. The world now, frankly, is driven by previews and scores, so whatever trouble I could have gotten into I dodged because it played.

Did you attend all of the preview screenings?
Of course. It's hair-raising. You have to, because the studio starts to quote to you what people in focus groups said, and you want to have heard it yourself just in case you need to argue. But the truth was that the studio loved this movie, long before any previews. Lucy Fischer and Amy Pascal, and John Calley, all of whom saw the movie the very first time I showed it, responded very strongly to it. And all the other executives – the head of marketing, the head of distribution – loved it, and at a big studio they are all so

important because they each control these separate wings.

Also, the funny thing was that, in a studio context, *Girl, Interrupted* was one of their cheapest movies. So that where *CopLand* for Miramax was a giant tentpole movie of the year, at this studio we were a kind of a lark. If we didn't spend too much, they'd leave us alone. They were making movies like *Godzilla* and *Starship Troopers*, whose budgets were many multiples of what we were spending. I'm sure they had a lot of trepidation about making this picture, and I do believe they showed a lot of courage and faith in Cathy and me and the cast in letting us go off to Harrisburg, Pennsylvania to make it. But we weren't their biggest fish, and that was a kind of a blessing.

Could you classify this movie for me? You've referenced every genre from war films to monster movies to love stories as your inspirations.
I always sort of thought to myself, 'This is a woman's picture with balls.' Instead of that kind of gauzy, pop-music-playing, gather-in-a-circle-and-talk-about-how-fucked-up-men-are kind of movie. What I think is so interesting about the movie is that it has incredible darkness and grit, but also such love, and it's so sweet. *Heavy*'s a pretty damn sweet movie, and I wanted to bring some of those energies to bear on the film. But also Winona, and a lot of the other women, brought such light and tenderness with them. I think it's a very unique combination of grit and terror and darkness and a kind of love. So in that sense it still is a classical woman's drama, but at the same time it does try to get to the nugget of some other deep stuff.

What are you working on now?
I'm doing a rewrite on a romantic comedy. It's a story about love and destiny and time travel, and I'm trying to write it in a very amped-up style – I'm looking at a lot of Preston Sturges, and trying to learn a lot from him about how fast you can keep everything moving. It's been a kind of release of pressure from the heaviness of this film. I'm not sure I want to do another picture just like this again, although I do very much enjoy the fact that I can make dramas in the Hollywood context. For so many young directors, we're kind of cordoned off in the world of being big shooters of action pictures or doing kind of quirky independent movies, or else the third thing, teen pictures. But I'm really

honored to be getting the chance to be working in the genre of Martin Ritt, or Sidney Lumet, or Mike Nichols. That I managed to get my foot in that door is really amazing. But I'm trying to keep jumping around, and I think Cathy's a great adviser on that. Early on, don't let anyone pin you down. It's always about protecting yourself. I don't know what's going to happen with this movie, but as long as I keep jumping around, no one's quite sure. Maybe this one's a very commercial picture, maybe the next one's a very commercial picture. But as long as I keep dancing and shadowboxing, no one can fix me as the guy that makes the one kind of movie that no one wants to see.

Girl, Interrupted

1968. Dawn. Wind rattles frosted glass.

Looking out an open transom. Through steel mesh.

Brown grass. Barren trees. A spider crawls across the mesh.

We pan. We are in a dark tiled basement.

The sound of a cat purring. And a person breathing.

We pan. Past rusting pipes. *Drip. Drop.*

A furnace. Licking flame behind sooty glass. *Foosssh.*

We pan. Past a cracked journal. An endless word-stream:
*A ship without a rudder
is like a ship without a rudder
is like a ship without a rudder*

Sunlight hits a puddle. A hypodermic glistens.

Light ripples. Susanna's eyes. They fill the screen.

Big. Brown. Racooned with exhaustion. Grease-smudged.

One of her hands. Bloody. Curled against her chest.

The other hand moves. Petting an unseen cat.

It purrs. We move down. It is *not* a cat.

It is another young woman. Blonde. Lazy-eyed.

Her head in Susanna's lap. She purrs.

Purrs with every stroke of her yellow hair.

The tinkle of broken glass. Susanna turns.

A red-haired girl sweeps glass and mutters in a sing-song a song
from *The Wizard of Oz.*

Footsteps *echo.* Heels. *Loud.*

Down the hall of pipes. A flashlight. Figures approach.

A black woman in a nurse's uniform. And an orderly.

Behind the furnace. Blue eyes rise in fear.

Blue watery eyes set in a face of curdled leather.

It is a girl – horribly scarred – crying in the shadows. Her mittened hands wrapped around a gray cat. A real cat.

Susanna watches the burnt girl. Her voice is lush. Calm:

> SUSANNA
> (voice-over)
> People ask how we got in there.
> What they really want to know is if
> they're likely to end up there as well.

Dawn light caresses Susanna's face. *A phasing whir rises.*

> I can't answer the real question.
> All I can tell you is . . . *it's easy.*

SUDDENLY, WHITE HANDS GRAB SUSANNA'S HEAD –

> *It's easy to enter a parallel universe.*

TWO OTHER HANDS THRUST A TUBE UP HER NOSE, DOWN HER THROAT, PUSHING HER FACE DOWNWARDS – TO A STRETCHER. WHITE LIGHT.

WE ARE: IN A BRIGHT 60S EMERGENCY ROOM – NIGHT

A PALE SUSANNA RIDES A MOVING STRETCHER. IT SCREECHES TO A STOP. *A tube is inserted. A 'lavage' pump whirs on and SUSANNA* VOMITS IN A BASIN. SHE'S ROLLED ON HER BACK. EERILY CONSCIOUS. She pulls at the tubes, tries to sit up, *gagging.*

> SUSANNA
> – I'm okay –

> NURSE
> – *hold on, dear* –

> ER DOCTOR
> (off-screen)
> Five milligrams Valium. *Restrain her* –

THE NURSE FASTENS RESTRAINTS. *The pump continues sending water down Susanna's throat.* SHE CHOKES, PULLS THE STRAPS.

> SUSANNA
> *Ow.*

A NEEDLE PRICKS HER ARM – A NURSE *DRAWS OUT BLOOD.*
ANOTHER NEEDLE – A NURSE INJECTS VALIUM.

> *OW!*

A RESIDENT takes the basin and examines the contents. IT IS
FILLED WITH PILL FRAGMENTS. CLEAR LIQUID. He leans toward
the ER DOCTOR.

> RESIDENT
> Aspirin fragments and vodka, I think.

> ER DOCTOR
> Don't tell me what you think. Take it upstairs.

Susanna looks to A CONCERNED MAN (forty-five) IN THE CORNER.
Arms crossed, he wears a tweedy vest and has a goatee.

The lavage pump winds down and the DOCTOR pulls the tube. He
takes Susanna's tongue in his fingers – brusque. Susanna gags,
looking helplessly into his eyes.

> SUSANNA
> *– eee's iiigh –*

The Doctor does not react – he releases her tongue and spreads
her fingers, looking closely at them.

> NURSE
> What did you say, dear?

The Doctor checks her arms, notices *A BRUISE ON HER WRIST.*

> ER DOCTOR
> *A wrist-banger.*

> SUSANNA
> I said, he's right – *it's aspirin.*

ER DOCTOR
(moving to her legs)
I still have to check for track marks, young lady. Any signs of
drug abuse.
(looking up, smiling grimly)
Attempted suicide is a *felony*.

SUSANNA
(head heavy, to Nurse)
– really – whas the punishment –

NURSE
Your parents are on the way.

SUSANNA
(downright stoned now)
– He sho *–* look at my *hand*.
There's no bones in it.

ER DOCTOR
Is that why you did this?
Because there's no bones in your hand?

SUSANNA glances at THE MAN IN TWEED. He shifts, nervous.

SUSANNA
– and other things – it's hard to stay *– for me –* to stay in one
place.

There is an off-screen voice:

VOICE
Susanna. If you had no bones in your hand *–*

SUSANNA TURNS, GROGGY (TO FACE THE VOICE) AND WE

CUT TO:

DR CRUMBLE: A SHRINK IN HIS FIFTIES

DR CRUMBLE
– how did you pick up the aspirin?

HE SITS IN A COMFY CHAIR, AWAITING AN ANSWER.

REVERSE ON: SUSANNA, dark-eyed, in a less comfy chair. She wears a turtleneck and a mini. HER SLENDER ARM bounces – *fuff fuff fuff* – on the plastic covered armrest. The fabric below, tangerine. *There's a bandage on her wrist.* We're in an office in a suburban house. *A car passes.* Susanna glances out the window. A WOMAN PULLS A SAMSONITE CASE from a Volvo.

                    SUSANNA
     What is my mother doing?

                    DR CRUMBLE
     Can you answer my question?

Susanna turns, facing him.

     How did you pick up the aspirin – *with no bones in your hand?*

                    SUSANNA
     By then they had come back.

                    DR CRUMBLE
     I see.

                    SUSANNA
     No. You don't.
                    (demure)
     It's beyond you.

She lights a cigarette. Her hand is shaking. She is holding back. The Doctor stares at her. Her eyes meet his. Angry.

                    DR CRUMBLE
                    (smiles)
     Indulge me. Explain it.

                    SUSANNA
     Explain *what* – explain to a *doctor* that the laws of physics can be suspended – that what goes up might not come down?

Somewhere – *a dog starts barking.*

     – explain that time can flow backward from now to then and back again – and that you can't control it?

7

                         DR CRUMBLE
      Why can't you control it?

THE DOG BARKS LOUDER. Classical music is heard in the distance.

                         SUSANNA
                    (distracted by the dog)
      . . . *what?*

                         DR CRUMBLE
      Why can't you control time?

SUSANNA TURNS TO FACE:

A FAMILY DOG BARKS AT SUSANNA — HALFWAY IN A KITCHEN
DOOR —

WE ARE: INT. KAYSEN HOUSE — NIGHT (FLASHBACK)

SUSANNA'S MOTHER (ANNETTE) rushes in. Colorfully dressed, she
holds a plate of hors d'oeuvres. *Classical music plays.*

                         ANNETTE
      Where were you? Everyone's here.

ANNETTE PULLS SUSANNA PAST HER FATHER, CHATTING WITH
SOMEONE —

                         SUSANNA
      Hey, Daddy . . .

— INTO A LIVING ROOM PACKED WITH GUESTS.

                         ANNETTE
      Look who's here, everybody!

EVERYONE LOOKS UP — offers greetings.

MRS GILCREST, a well-meaning lady wearing macramé, reacts to
Susanna's arrival. She stands, handing her husband, PROFESSOR
GILCREST (forty-five), a drink. *He wears a tweed vest and has a
goatee.*

                         MRS GILCREST
      Babe, can you hold this for me?

8

> (rushing Susanna)
I want to say hello.

                         ANNETTE
                  (hushed, to Susanna)
Professor Gilcrest's wife.

From across the room PROFESSOR GILCREST LEERS AT SUSANNA.
Susanna rubs her head, leans in to her mother's ear.

                         SUSANNA
Do we have aspirin down here? I need to go upstai–

                         MRS GILCREST
My Lord! What beautiful skin! You remember me, don't you?
Barbara Gilcrest, Bonnie's mom. Bonnie was in your Lit
class, wasn't she?

                         SUSANNA
Yeah. How's she doing?

                         MRS GILCREST
'Just accepted at Radcliffe. What a conundrum. I'm a
Wellesley girl myself, but these days young women should
make up their own minds, *don't you think*?

THE PROFESSOR CONTINUES STARING. SUSANNA AVERTS HER
EYES.

Where are you headed this fall?

                         DR CRUMBLE
                       (off-screen)
Susanna. Are you stoned?

SUSANNA LOOKS BACK UP – BEWILDERED. (BACK TO PRESENT)

She is facing DR CRUMBLE.

                         DR CRUMBLE
Do you smoke pot? Take LSD?

THE ASH ON HER TREMBLING CIGARETTE. It is two inches long.

No drugs?

9

SUSANNA
(taps her ash)
I find them redundant.

DR CRUMBLE
Have a boyfriend? Maybe a few.
(smiles)
Older boyfriends?

Susanna smiles, knowingly.

How do you feel right now?

SUSANNA
'like you're getting hopeful.

The Doctor shifts in his chair. Unswerved.

DR CRUMBLE
Is that all you're feeling? *What else?*

Susanna looks him in the eye. *Defiant. The truth.*

SUSANNA
I – don't – know. I don't know what I'm feeling.

DR CRUMBLE
You need a rest.

SUSANNA
I'll go home . . . take a nap.

DR CRUMBLE
No. You need to go somewhere where you can get genuine
rest, Susanna. And you're lucky – because the best place in
the world for someone like yourself happens to be a half-hour
from here.

SUSANNA
You don't mean Claymoore.

Dr Crumble says nothing.

That's a bit extreme, isn't it?

Susanna rolls her eyes.

DR CRUMBLE

Extreme? Four days ago, you chased a bottle of aspirin with a bottle of vodka.

SUSANNA

I had a headache.

DR CRUMBLE

Susanna. Your father is a friend of mine. A colleague. He asked me to see you –

Susanna glances at CRUMBLE'S FACE ON THE BACK OF A NEARBY BOOK JACKET. An important-looking tome entitled *The Mind.*

– even though I don't do this anymore, he *begged* me to see you. He's frightened. So is your mother. You are hurting everyone around you. Claymoore is *top-notch.* Many people have gone there. Writers – *like you.*

SUSANNA

Whatever.

Susanna looks off. Crumble rises, pleased. Dials a phone.

DR CRUMBLE

Yes. Can I get a cab at 1240 Milford?

SUSANNA

My mom is here.

DR CRUMBLE
(covering the receiver)
It's less emotional this way. Your parents and I discussed this.

CUT TO:

EXT./INT. SUBURBAN HOUSE/CAB – DAY – AUTUMN

DOCTOR CRUMBLE leads SUSANNA by the elbow toward A CAB. Susanna notices HER SAMSONITE CASE in the back.

Down the block, HER MOTHER cries in the Volvo.

> DR CRUMBLE
> (handing the driver cash)

No stops.

His face looms large as he closes the door.

> *Bye bye.*

The cab takes off, rumbling. Susanna's mother's Volvo becomes a speck.

Susanna turns back. Lighting a cigarette. *The cab radio chimes the hour. News headlines read aloud: Escalating fighting in Nam. Civil Rights riots.* Susanna notices:

THE CAB DRIVER'S WILD EYES. Meeting hers in the rear-view. Long-haired, bearded. He looks like Charles Manson. She looks to THE DRIVER'S ID CARD mounted on the dash: IT IS ON A PHOTO – the man is clean-shaven. But still wild-eyed. His name: M O N T Y   H O O V E R. *The sound of people singing a muffled 'Happy Birthday'. And someone knocking on a door.* SUSANNA TURNS TO FACE:

A BEDROOM DOOR. *SOMEONE KNOCKS AGAIN – LIGHTLY.*

WE ARE: INT. SUSANNA'S BEDROOM – NIGHT (FLASHBACK)

In her nightie, SUSANNA opens the door a crack. Standing there is PROFESSOR GILCREST. Drunk. *He whispers over the singing downstairs.*

> PROFESSOR GILCREST

I want to see you again.

> SUSANNA

It was a one-time thing.

> PROFESSOR GILCREST

Come to the office later. Please. Tell them you're going to a friend's.

> SUSANNA

Who do I tell first? My parents, the department chairman, *or your wife?*

Susanna closes the door, locks it. *A siren rises.*
She winces, leans her head against the door.
THE SIREN GETS LOUDER; a strange triad of notes.

SUSANNA OPENS HER EYES – SHE IS IN THE CAB (BACK TO
PRESENT)

PASSING BY THE WINDOW: AN AMBULANCE AT AN ACCIDENT
SITE. People mill about a body on a stretcher.

On the radio, Van Morrison: 'It's all over now, Baby Blue'. Susanna
checks her ash. It is two inches long.

MONTY THE CAB DRIVER looks at her.
They are stuck in Boston traffic. SUSANNA NOTICES:

AMID A BEATNIK CROWD, A LONG-LIMBED GIRL stands on the
shoulder, amid traffic, smoking a cigarette. She wears ragged
cuffed jeans and a T-shirt. HER LAZY EYES MEET:

SUSANNA, WHO TURNS AWAY. OUT THE OTHER WINDOW AN
IDENTICAL BOSTON CAB idles in traffic, facing the opposite
direction.

SUSANNA STARES, FASCINATED. In the back of the 'mirror cab' she
sees HERSELF. A DOPPELGANGER. Sitting there. Going home.
Smoking. Traffic breaks and the cab pulls away.
SUSANNA sighs, pressing her wrist on the armrest. She flops down
across the back seat, propping her head on her case.
SHE STARES UPWARD. *The unnerving music builds as we:*

CUT TO:

LEAF-LACED MOONLIGHT SWIRLING ON THE CEILING.
Music cross-fades to off-screen voices. Goodbyes. Party's over.

WE ARE: INT. SUSANNA'S ROOM – NIGHT (FLASHBACK)

SUSANNA LIES WIDE AWAKE IN BED. STARING AT THE CEILING.
The shadows on the ceiling form a face. A man with a goatee?
Gilcrest? It becomes a *demon. A guy laughs downstairs.*

Susanna feels something – looks down and brings her hand to her
face. Suddenly, she's horrified, stricken, staring at:

HER HAND IN THE MOONLIGHT. As she flexes it, her fingers bend *backwards*, the knuckles popping. *More laughing downstairs.*
SUSANNA SWALLOWS A SCREAM AND RUNS OUT THE DOOR.

                                                    CUT TO:

A BATHROOM DOOR LOCKS. *FLUORESCENT FLICKER ON:*

In her nightie, SUSANNA stands in the pulsing light.
She stares into the mirror. HER HAND IS NORMAL.
The doorknob jiggles. *Someone's trying to get in.*

                         SUSANNA
     I'm fine!

The doorknob jiggles again. Susanna flings open the door.

     I'M *FINE!*

There is no one in the hall. Down the staircase, HER PARENTS AND
GUESTS (the Gilcrests among them) look up from goodbyes.
Susanna covers her face, tortured, and turns back to the
bathroom, closes her eyes, then opens them upon:
A BOTTLE OF ASPIRIN on the sink in the flickering light.

                    CAB DRIVER (MONTY)
                        (off-screen)
     What did you do?

SUSANNA SITS UP WITH A START.

WE ARE BACK: INT./EXT. CAB TO CLAYMOORE – DAY (PRESENT)

THE DRIVER (MONTY) watches her curiously. They are driving
down a country road. He asks her again:

                         MONTY
     What did you do?

                         SUSANNA
     Excuse me?

                         MONTY
     You look normal.

Susanna smiles politely.

                           14

Passing outside – children play in a leaf pile, laughing.

> SUSANNA

– I'm sad.

> MONTY

Big deal. Everyone's sad.

> SUSANNA

I see things.

> MONTY

You mean, like, tripping?

> SUSANNA

Kind of.

> MONTY

Well, then they better put John Lennon away, huh?

> SUSANNA
> (smiles at the thought)

I'm not John Lennon.

> MONTY

Maybe that's why you're sad.

Monty turns the wheel. They enter a winding campus road.

THE SIGN READS: *CLAYMOORE*. A GROUP OF WARM AND
GRACIOUS BUILDINGS, which could be part of a college.
Monty pulls to a stop in front of A HANDSOME BRICK BUILDING.
A NURSE approaches. She has a cool Afro and a confident walk, a
strut. She opens the cab door. HER NAME TAG READS: *VALERIE*.

> VALERIE

Susanna?

Monty turns around, looks Susanna in the eye.

> MONTY

Don't get too comfortable.

                                    CUT TO:

INT. ADMINISTRATION LOBBY AND STAIRS – DAY

Wide-eyed, Susanna passes GUARDS following VALERIE, who takes Susanna's Samsonite and moves briskly up varnished stairs.

> VALERIE
> Dr Cornish is giving you a check-up, and then we'll sign you in up at Dr Wick's office. I'm Valerie, by the way. I'm in charge of your ward.

> CUT TO:

INT. ADMINISTRATION – EXAMINATION ROOM – DAY

SUSANNA sits in a gown on a vinyl-padded table.

She pulls on a loose thread as DR CORNISH listens to her heart with a stethoscope.
VALERIE sits by the door with a fashion magazine.

> CUT TO:

INT. DR WICK'S OUTER OFFICE – DAY

CLOSE ON: SUSANNA. BLEARY AS SHE EXAMINES ADMITTANCE FORMS:

> *I, Susanna Kaysen, hereby commit myself . . .*
> *. . . understand I will not be released from care until . . .*

> SUSANNA
> I thought my parents –

A WHITE-HAIRED LADY (ARLEEN) SMILES CONDESCENDINGLY.

> ARLEEN
> *You* have to sign them, Miss Kaysen.
> *You're over eighteen. This is your decision.*

A NAMEPLATE ON THE OFFICE DOOR READS: S. G. WICK, MD. INSIDE AN OBSCURED PERSON IN A WHITE COAT COUGHS. VALERIE STANDS OUTSIDE THE DOOR, READING ANOTHER MAGAZINE.

                    SUSANNA
I didn't try to kill myself.

                    ARLEEN
That's the kind of thing you talk about in *therapy*, honey. Not
here.

SUSANNA looks to Valerie. SHE SIGNS THE ADMITTANCE FORMS.

                    MISS PAISLEY
                    (off-screen)
Miss Kaysen, you have the distinction –

SUSANNA LOOKS UP TO FACE:

MISS PAISLEY, A WHITE-HAIRED GUIDANCE COUNSELOR looks
through a file. A BOTTLE OF ASPIRIN SITS ON HER DESK.

    – of being the only Senior at Springbrook *not* going on to
    college.

WE ARE: INT. GUIDANCE COUNSELOR'S OFFICE – DAY
(FLASHBACK)

Susanna presses her wrist, staring at the aspirin.

                    SUSANNA
Um. Do you have any aspirin?

The woman hands Susanna the bottle. Susanna swallows a
handful of tablets, washes it with a Coke.

                    MISS PAISLEY
May I ask what you plan to do?

                    SUSANNA
I don't have a plan.

                    MISS PAISLEY
Everyone has a plan.

                    SUSANNA
I plan to write.

But what do you plan to *do*?

SUSANNA

You mean like: *a) get married or b) go to college and get married.*

Miss Paisley smiles, strained. Susanna tries to be sincere:

Look. I'm not gonna burn my bra or drop acid or march on Washington. I just don't want to be my mother, alright?

MISS PAISLEY

Women today have more choices than that.

SUSANNA

No, they don't.

MISS PAISLEY

Have you thought about taking a secretarial course? Or volunteering as a student nurse?

Susanna laughs. She looks away. Miss Paisley becomes stern:

It's not funny. It would buy you some time, Susanna. We all have to grow up and do *something*. It may not be *everything* we hoped for but we have to wake up everyday and *do something useful* with ourselves or else – *what's the point?*

Susanna looks up.

ARLEEN
(off-screen)

. . . and here.

BACK TO:

ARLEEN IN DR WICK'S OUTER OFFICE (BACK TO PRESENT)

Arleen points out a place on the form SUSANNA missed.

ARLEEN

You forgot one, dear. Here.

Susanna signs and pushes the papers across to Arleen.

Well. Speaking for Dr Wick and myself, welcome to Claymoore, Susanna.

                              SUSANNA
     Thanks. It doesn't look so bad.

THE UNSEEN DR WICK COUGHS AGAIN from inside his office.

                              ARLEEN
     What did you expect?

                              SUSANNA
     I don't know. Bars on the windows. Screaming crazies.

                              ARLEEN
     Well, fortunately, it's a private hospital, so we have –

                              SUSANNA
     – *a lot of rich patients.*

                              ARLEEN
     – *the resources* to maintain a healing atmosphere.

                                                    CUT TO:

EXT. APPROACHING SOUTH BELL – DAY

VALERIE leads SUSANNA briskly along a RAISED WALKWAY past
several brick buildings. A GROUP OF MEN PLAY VOLLEYBALL in
the distance. Susanna notices:

TRANSOMS run at ground level along the edges of the sidewalk. *A
GARDENER passes sacks of mulch up through one of them.*

                              VALERIE
     Tunnels under the walkways. From the old days. They
     connect every building on campus.

Susanna nods. Valerie OPENS THE MAIN DOOR TO A LARGER
BRICK BUILDING MARKED 'SOUTH BELL'.

     The Women's Ward – South Bell – where I work and where
     you'll be staying.

                                                    CUT TO:

INT. SOUTH BELL – MOVING – HALL/STAIRS – DAY

SUSANNA finds herself facing:

A LONG DARK HALL through a wall of thick wire mesh. VALERIE UNLOCKS A SIDE DOOR LEADING TO A STAIRCASE.

> VALERIE

This way.

Susanna follows Valerie, spiraling upward. The staircase also encased in thick mesh. On the landing, Valerie unlocks ANOTHER DOOR, leading into:

INT. SOUTH BELL – THE WARD – DAY

A LONG HALL WITH A GREAT ROUND WINDOW AT ONE END. The sound of squealing girls echoes down the hall. Figures move about at the far end. Susanna's eyes are wide. She takes a few steps down the hall, taking it all in.

Valerie crosses to unlock a door but discovers it's open.

> VALERIE

God-dammit, Margie.
> (noticing Susanna wandering)

Stay with me, baby.

Valerie opens the door to a LARGE LIGHT-FILLED ROOM with crude artwork on the walls, and supplies behind thick mesh.

Pling! In a side nook, A YOUNG GIRL, her back turned, stands before an array of MUSICAL INSTRUMENTS, also locked up. She strains against the mesh, trying to pluck a guitar string.

Polly, what are you doing in here?!

The young girl (POLLY) turns, revealing she's a seriously scarred burn victim (the leather-faced girl of the opening scene). Her sweet eyes make strange counterpoint to the horrific texture of her face. She runs out of the room and Valerie smiles at Susanna, speaking matter-of-factly:

The art room. You'll be painting and sculpting in here. Arts and crafts.

> SUSANNA

. . . Great.

Valerie locks the door and leads Susanna down the hall. Polly now stands before them, walking backwards.

POLLY

Valerie?

VALERIE

Yes, Polly.

POLLY

I feel musical today. Can we?

VALERIE

Not today.

Polly accepts this cheerfully and flits into a room.

Susanna peers in doorways as they move, catching glimpses of:

A GIRL IN HER ROOM, SMOKING, READING A FASHION MAGAZINE.

ANOTHER GIRL DANCING ABOUT IN HER ROOM AS THEY PASS.

THEY APPROACH A YOUNG NURSE (MARGIE) with a meds tray.

Art room was wide open, Margie.

MARGIE

I'm sorry, Val. I'll talk to Gretta.

Valerie moves on, pointing out A LARGE ROOM off the hall. Fancy wallpaper. Antique furniture. Like a funeral parlour. *No one is there* except ONE OLDER GIRL KNITTING A LONG SCARF.

VALERIE

The living room. Everyone hates it.

Valerie continues down the hall past THREE PHONE BOOTHS.

The phones. If you want to call someone, you pick up a phone, a nurse answers, and you tell her who you want to call.

A sticker in one of the phone booths reads:
IF YOU LIVED HERE, YOU'D BE HOME NOW. Susanna winces.

Valerie nods to A CHAMBER ENCLOSED IN REINFORCED GLASS.
A YOUNG NURSE works inside. Valerie hands her coat to her.

Nurses' station. Self-explanatory.

DAISY, a conservative, Patricia Nixon-type, peers out of her door,
which has a sign tacked on it reading: *NO TRESPASSING*.
Compelling, taut and sexy, she watches Susanna.

A few steps further, the hall opens up into:

A LARGE SUNNY ROOM. A TV SQUAWKS IN THE CENTER. With
vinyl armchairs and couches, and card tables. TWO CATATONICS
are (not) watching *FATHER KNOWS BEST*. One older with a fifties
hairstyle. The other, in her teens, with a perpetually startled
expression. JANET (seventeen), a green-eyed anorexic, gets up
from doing extensions. Skin and bones, she wears a hospital gown
and sucks a cig, looking piercingly at Valerie.

The TV room. Most girls hang out here.

> JANET
> I want my fucking *clothes*!

> VALERIE
> And when you break eighty, you'll get them, Janet.

Valerie moves on, but SUSANNA LINGERS, looking back as:

JANET FLICKS AN ASH IN A CATATONIC'S MOUTH and sings a
refrain from *Porgy and Bess*, trying to annoy Valerie.

Valerie ignores her, smiling to Susanna, moving on:

She thinks that bothers me.

Valerie stands before A LARGE BLACKBOARD near A DISPENSARY.
The board is filled with patient names, privileges and space to fill
in destinations, times out and in.

Here you sign in or out – if you want to take a walk on the
grounds, for instance.

Janet is still singing Porgy and Bess, *on her knees now.*
Susanna tries to focus on the names on the blackboard. Among

them: *Daisy, Polly, Georgina, Janet, Cynthia and Lisa.* Susanna's name is at the bottom, with an 'R' next to it.

> Right now, you're 'R', restricted. You can't go beyond the ward. But after you've been a month, *you'll* move to 'two to ones'; two nurses to one patient.

                    SUSANNA
I'm sure I won't be here that long. I'm just here for a rest.

Valerie smiles, moving on down the hall.

                    VALERIE
Everyone gets the same tour, no charge.

MORE GIRLS CHECK SUSANNA OUT. *AMONG THEM:*

CYNTHIA: crew cut, would now be called a lesbian.
THE MARTIAN'S GIRLFRIEND: grinning through bad teeth.
POLY: we saw her before. The sweet-faced burn victim.

AT THE END OF THE HALL, VALERIE OPENS THE DOOR TO:
A SMALL ROOM. A MATTRESS LIES ON A GREEN LINOLEUM FLOOR.

> The seclusion room. You come here any time you need to yell.

Susanna, pale, looks to:

Valerie, who turns, heading toward another room.

> By the way, if you don't feel like yelling, but you feel like talking, you let me know.
>   (beat, looking back)
> *While you're here.*

                                        CUT TO:

INT. SOUTH BELL – SUSANNA AND GEORGINA'S ROOM – DAY

SUSANNA AND VALERIE stop in front of a pleasant room, something between a college dorm and a colonial hotel room.

                    VALERIE
And this is your room.

23

On one of the small beds is GEORGINA, a red-haired all-American-looking girl of nineteen. (We saw her in the opening under more stress.) She's reading *The Patchwork Girl of Oz*.

Georgina, this is Susanna – your new *room-mate*.

GEORGINA

Oh, great! Hi. No kidding.

SUSANNA

Hi.

VALERIE

You got lucky, Susanna. Georgina is an excellent room-mate.

GEORGINA

Why thanks, Valerie.

Georgina smiles, laughs. Then, back to her book.

YOUNG NURSE
(off-screen)

Valerie.

A YOUNG NURSE (LILLIAN) appears in the door, concerned. She whispers something to Valerie, who turns around to Susanna.

VALERIE

There's something I need to attend to.

Susanna nods, hesitant.

Georgina, will you take Susanna to the dining room in ten minutes?

GEORGINA

Sure.

VALERIE
(moving off, cautioning)

Yes means yes, Georgina.

GEORGINA

I know.

This last exchange a mystery to Susanna. She simply smiles at Georgina and crosses to her Samsonite case on the second bed.

SHE POPS IT OPEN. A PRETTY DRESS AND PAJAMAS are folded on top. Susanna sighs at the inappropriateness of her mother's packing. She digs. Finds her red-covered JOURNAL. And A CARTON OF FRENCH CIGARETTES. AND SOME BETTER CLOTHES.

Pretty box.

SUSANNA
They're French. The French Resistance smoked them.

Georgina nods. Susanna opens a pack, pulls a cigarette.

You have a light? They took my matches.

GEORGINA
Nurses are supposed to light cigarettes.

Susanna lies back on the bed. Takes in the room. Dark spots on the wall and pieces of yellowed Scotch tape.

SUSANNA
Who was your room-mate before me?

Georgina ignores the question – then, suddenly, she looks up.

GEORGINA
(indicating her book)
Have you read this?

SUSANNA
No, but I saw the movie a bunch of times.

Susanna notices THE BOOKSHELF IS LINED WITH 'OZ' BOOKS: *The Wizard of Oz. Road to Oz. Ozma of Oz. Glinda of Oz, etc.*

GEORGINA
The movie's based on the first book. I read that, too. But there's no ruby slippers. They added that. This takes place afterward. Dorothy doesn't have such a big part in this one.

There is the bleat of a siren outside.

Susanna crosses to the meshed window.

Did you see *The Yellow Submarine*?

A POLICE CAR IS PARKED AT THE CURB. VALERIE ARRIVES.

(off-screen)
Did you notice *The Yellow Submarine* is just a cartoon *Wizard of Oz*? Instead of a yellow brick road, it's a *submarine*.

ONE OF THE POLICE OFFICERS opens the back door of the squad car, extends his hand to help out THE PASSENGER.

Georgina looks out her window. She becomes nervous.

Oh, *no*.

THE PASSENGER, A LONG-LIMBED GIRL, exits unassisted. Her hands are cuffed. She shakes her tangled mane of hair. The police remove her handcuffs and hand her over to Valerie.

INT. SOUTH BELL — MAIN HALLWAY

SUSANNA AND GEORGINA *peer out their door as:*

THE LONG-LIMBED GIRL WALKS DOWN THE HALLWAY WITH VALERIE.
Though filthy, there's a nobility to this girl, a poise.
OTHER GIRLS STAND IN THEIR DOORWAYS, WATCHING AS THEY PASS.

LONG-LIMBED GIRL
Hey, Torch!

POLLY chirps back, with a southern lilt:

POLLY
Hey, Lisa.

LISA
– you miss me?

POLLY
Not much.

Lisa and Valerie stop at the nurses' station.

VALERIE

Give me the hair thing.

LISA removes A FEATHER ROACH CLIP from her hair.

LISA

Hey Daisy! Let anyone in your room yet?

DAISY slams her door: *'NO TRESPASSING'*.

LISA'S EYES TRAVEL TO: SUSANNA AND GEORGINA
The sight of Susanna disturbs Lisa.

Who's that – with Georgie Girl?

Valerie says nothing, removing Lisa's belt.

Where's Maddy?

Suddenly, GEORGINA CLOSES THE DOOR cutting off Lisa's glare.

INT. GEORGINA AND SUSANNA'S ROOM

Georgina turns to Susanna. Desperate.

GEORGINA

I – can't deal with this.

WE HEAR VALERIE SHOUTING. SUDDENLY, THE DOOR BURSTS
OPEN. LISA – *eyes blazing* – raises her finger toward Susanna.

LISA

Who are you?

Susanna backs up toward her bed. Georgina stammers.

GEORGINA

Sh-she just got here, Lisa. Her name is Susanna. She smokes
French cigarettes.

LISA TAKES ONE OF HER SHOES AND THRUSTS IT UNDER THE DOOR,
kicking it. PEOPLE IMMEDIATELY ARRIVE AT THE DOOR, BANGING
ON IT. It's jammed but it won't hold. Lisa advances on Susanna.

LISA

I'm confused. Where THE FUCK is Madeline? What is your
SHIT doing all over HER BED?

SUSANNA

I don't know what you're talking about.

VALERIE bursts in the room. AN ORDERLY AND NURSE behind her.

VALERIE

Lisa – *Get out*! You've been gone two weeks. Shit has gone down since then.

Lisa spins around, glaring at Valerie. Her eyes are wild – possessed by the devil. She screams at the top of her lungs:

LISA

WHERE IS MADDY? WHERE THE FUCK IS MADDY?!

This outburst affects OTHER GIRLS in the hall. A catatonic head-bangs. Another cries. Another (MARTIAN'S GIRLFRIEND – M-G) begins to shout with Lisa. NURSES shepherd them to their rooms.

THE ORDERLY – JOHN – a sweet Irish boy, advances on Lisa.

VALERIE

You come with us NOW!

LISA'S EYES DART ACROSS THE FACES AROUND HER. It's at this moment that she understands – *Madeline is dead.* Like a cougar, Lisa leaps across the bed, grabbing Susanna by the collar, pointing her red-nailed finger at her face.

LISA

HOW'D SHE DO IT? *HOW – DID – SHE – DO – IT?! TALK – CAN YOU FUCKIN' TALK!?*

SUSANNA

I don't know!

VALERIE AND JOHN GRAB AT LISA BUT – SHE GOES WILD. SCREAMING, POINTING HER FINGER AT SUSANNA.

LISA

I will kill you, Geisha Girl.

THEY WRESTLE HER OUT INTO – THE HALLWAY

Shrieking. Kicking. LISA CLAWS VALERIE WITH LONG RED NAILS.

VALERIE

Damn. We have to cut those.

Susanna rises from behind her bed. She goes to the door –
STUDENT NURSES SIT ON LISA TO KEEP HER DOWN.

A HYPODERMIC IS HANDED TO VALERIE, spouting a clear liquid. It
is plunged into Lisa's shoulder. LISA SCREAMS in protest.

LISA

NO! No, no, *no* . . .

She melts. Goes dull-eyed. They pull Lisa to her feet. Orderlies
drag her to the last room – *the seclusion room.*

SUSANNA steps back into her room, pale. She looks to Georgina,
awaiting an explanation. Georgina methodically straightens the
wrinkles on her bed.

SUSANNA

Maddy was your room-mate?

No response. Georgina neatens her bookshelf, hums.

POLLY
(off-screen)

Maddy was Lisa's friend –

POLLY STANDS IN THE DOOR. She cocks her head at Susanna, her
waxy face stretched into a smile. Georgina hums louder.

– *and* Georgina's room-mate. It's short for Madeline. She was
sad last week – 'cause Lisa ran away. So she hanged herself
with the volley-ball net – from that light.

CUT TO:

INT. CLAYMOORE – DINING ROOM – NIGHT

Five girls at each table, dining on china with plastic forks. Patients
from other wards dine in separate sections.

SUSANNA SITS WITH POLLY AND GEORGINA who is still quiet.

JANET and M-G sit at an adjacent table. M-G is small, round and

29

often in contact with invisible friends. She eats from Janet's plate. CYNTHIA gets seconds of Jell-O. Due to her crew cut and boxy clothes, she stands out. She sits with Janet and M-G.

> POLLY
> That's Cynthia. She's here 'cause her parents don't like her clothes. That's Janet – she won't eat anything. And next to her is M-G, the Martian's Girlfriend.

DAISY moves past. She elbows another girl out of the way to get to the coffee pot. She glances at Susanna.

> And that's Daisy. She's got her own room. Her daddy pays extra for that.

Daisy sits down alone, sipping her coffee. She looks nauseous and shields her eyes from all the eating going on around her.

> DAISY
> *Can someone get me a fucking light?*

Susanna meets eyes with JOHN THE ORDERLY, who lights Daisy's cigarette. M-G leans over to Susanna.

> MARTIAN'S GIRLFRIEND
> I have a penis. Want to see it?

> SUSANNA
> Um . . . can I have a light?

John lights Susanna's cigarette.

> JOHN
> You okay? *Susanna, right?*

Susanna nods.

> *I'm John.*

He smiles and moves off.

> JANET
> What kind of cigarette is that?

> SUSANNA
> Gauloise.

Susanna has a perfect French accent.

                    JANET
  Go-what?

                    GEORGINA
  The French Resistance smoked them.
  They're very chic.

                    JANET
  You're gonna run out of *them*.

                    SUSANNA
  I'm not going to be here that long.
  I'm just here for a rest.

Janet looks at Georgina, knowingly.

                                        CUT TO:

INT. SOUTH BELL – OUTSIDE DISPENSARY – NIGHT

Susanna stands, smoking. *I Dream of Jeanie on TV.*

MRS MCWILLEY, a veteran nurse with gray hair that clings to her
head like a migraine, holds a tray filled with LITTLE PAPER CUPS.
She calls out the name of each girl and they come forward,
dutifully. *It is like a graduation ceremony.*

                    MRS MCWILLEY
  Susanna Kaysen?

Susanna stands, unsure – steps forward. McWilley smiles:

  Good evening, Susanna.
  I'm Mrs McWilley. And this is for you.

                    SUSANNA
  What is it?

                    MRS MCWILLEY
  It'll help you sleep.

                    SUSANNA
  But it's only ten-thirty. I don't –

DAISY

Oh, for Christ's sake.

Susanna looks to Polly, who happily swallows her pills.

MRS MCWILLEY

You can discuss it in the morning, dear – *with your doctor.* In the meantime, we'll just have to agree to disagree.

Susanna swallows the pills. She stands there, realizing she's now free to head back to the couch, her room, wherever.

AT THE END OF THE HALL – THE DOOR TO SECLUSION IS OPEN – TWO NURSES tend to LISA, a tangle of hair, strung out.

Susanna turns away, eyes fluttering. The drugs taking effect. At the other end of the hall, McWilley calls out more names, continuing this medicinal graduation ceremony: *We hear a band playing Pomp and Circumstance.*

Cynthia Crowley . . . Daisy Randazzo . . .

SUSANNA puts her hand on the wall, supporting herself.

CUT TO:

EXT. SCHOOL LAWN – DAY (FLASHBACK)

A graduation ceremony.

MOVING PAST – THE PARENTS: well-dressed, beaming – except for CARL AND ANNETTE KAYSEN, who look anxiously at –

SUSANNA – AMONG THE ROBED GRADUATES – FALLING ASLEEP. GROGGY.

TOBIAS JACOBS, a good-looking college guy with a pony-tail, sits with his family. He smiles, watching Susanna sleep.

THE PRINCIPAL is at the podium, calling out names.

PRINCIPAL

Andrea Jacobs. Yearbook Editor,
President of the French Society . . .

Andrea, next to Susanna, rises and steps over Susanna's feet.

    Susanna Kaysen . . .

Susanna remains asleep. A HUNDRED HEADS TURN, ALL FACING HER.

    Susanna Kaysen . . . ?

There is a strange silence. A ritual run aground.

Suddenly – *click, swish:*

THE DOOR TO SUSANNA AND GEORGINA'S ROOM FLINGS OPEN

SUSANNA OPENS HER EYES. A FLASHLIGHT-WIELDING STUDENT NURSE shines her light on Susanna, scaring the hell out of her.

> NURSE
> Checks.

The light sweeps over Georgina. She rolls over, half-asleep.

Swish, click: THE NURSE IS GONE.

All quiet again. Trees blowing.

> SUSANNA
> Georgina?

After a beat, Georgina opens her eyes – groggy.

    Why do they do that?

> GEORGINA
> *They're doing checks. They space'm out more after you've been a while.*

> SUSANNA
> I can't even *think.*

> GEORGINA
> That's the point.

> SUSANNA
> How did that girl – *Polly* – get all . . .

GEORGINA

When she was ten, her mommy told her she had to give away her puppy – he was giving her a rash. So Polly found her daddy's gas can, poured it all over – where she was getting the rash – and lit a match.

Susanna takes this in, horrified.

SUSANNA

. . . Why are *you* here?

GEORGINA

Pseudologia Fantastica.

SUSANNA

What's that?

GEORGINA

I'm a pathological liar.

Georgina smiles and closes her eyes. She lies very still now.

Susanna crosses to – THE DOOR. *The hall is quiet.* No sign of the Nurse. Just the throbbing light of the TV.

SUSANNA

I have to go to the bathroom.
Am I allowed? *Georgina.*
I don't know where it is.

Nothing. Georgina is out cold.

CUT TO:

INT. SOUTH BELL – HALLWAY – NIGHT

From somewhere, a cat meows.

The television flickers in the empty TV ROOM.

SUSANNA pads down the hallway. She approaches the door to *SECLUSION*. She peers in through the door's little window.

The room is dark, moonlit. The mattress is bare *and empty.* Susanna gets on her toes. Looks again. *But Lisa is not there. The big door creaks.* It's open. She pulls away, quickly.

34

Susanna moves the other way – up the hall.

The hallway splits. ARROWS point in both directions – *art room, administration, etc.* – but no mention of a bathroom.

> WOMAN'S VOICE
> (off-screen)
> You could go that way.

Susanna stiffens. A sluggish, drugged voice:

> *– or you could go the other way.*

Susanna spins around. The hall is empty.

> *Myself.* If I had to take a wee. I'd go to the third door on the right.

In the flickering light of the TV ROOM, LISA MEOWS. SUSANNA BOLTS – SPRINTING DOWN THE HALL.

> CUT TO:

INT. SOUTH BELL – BATHROOM – NIGHT

Blue tile. Green fluorescents. A morgue. Water drips.
THE STALL is covered with SEXUALLY GRAPHIC GRAFFITI.
Crudely drawn dicks. A primitive caricature of McWilley (spelled 'McWillie') rides one, blissful.

SUSANNA flushes the toilet. She is exposed (there are no doors), her eyes riveted on the entrance.

> CUT TO:

INT. SOUTH BELL – HALLWAY – NIGHT

SUSANNA walks briskly around the corner, past the TV room.
There's no one there. But there's an incessant stream of *meows* coming from the darkness. *The essence of madness.*

SUSANNA CHARGES DOWN THE HALLWAY, and rounding the corner, runs headlong into MRS MCWILLEY. *SUSANNA SCREAMS.*

> MRS MCWILLEY
> Next time, push the call button. Here's another sleepy pill.

35

SHE PUSHES A PINK PILL into Susanna's mouth.

CUT TO:

INT. SOUTH BELL — SUSANNA AND GEORGINA'S ROOM —
MORNING

SUSANNA sleeps in the dawn light. Pillow in her arms. GEORGINA
sits in bed, reading. A transistor radio on her pillow plays the
Chambers Brothers' 'Time Has Come Today'.

Suddenly, *click, swish:* THE DOOR FLINGS OPEN and there is
MARGIE, A STUDENT NURSE, with a clipboard.

MARGIE

Checks.

Susanna's eyes flutter. *Swish, click.* The door closes. She looks to
Georgina, who is oblivious. *Georgina's music drones on.* Susanna
rolls over, her eyes focusing on:

HERSELF — DANCING, IN PULSING LIGHT WITH A FRECKLED BOY
(JOSH).

WE ARE AT: A PARTY — A CAMBRIDGE APARTMENT — NIGHT
(FLASHBACK)

On the record-player, THE CHAMBERS BROTHERS *in glorious hi-fi.*
JOSH keeps coming closer to Susanna. He yells over the music.

JOSH

What are your plans for the fall?

SUSANNA

What?!

JOSH

What are your plans?!

SUSANNA

I don't have any.

JOSH

I'm going to be an ethnobotanist.

SUSANNA

I'm thinking of joining the *Krishna*.

JOSH

Hare Krishna? *That's interesting.*

SUSANNA

I was just kidding . . . *God.*

Susanna bolts away, crossing to the food table. She grabs a bottle
of wine and tries to pour but – IT SPILLS ON THE WHITE TABLE
CLOTH.

Shit!

She wipes at the SPREADING STAIN, feeling *Josh watching her.*

TOBIAS

(off-screen)

I hate parties.

Susanna turns around to see TOBIAS JACOBS (*the handsome young
man looking at her at graduation*).

SUSANNA

So do I.

TOBIAS

What do you hate most?

SUSANNA

The talking. The people. The general misery of Existence.

TOBIAS

I'm Toby, Andrea Jacob's brother. I was at graduation.

(smiles)

You're pretty when you sleep.

BACK TO:

Click. Swish. THE DOOR OF SUSANNA'S ROOM OPENS.

LILLIAN

Checks. Seven o'clock.

Swish, click. The door closes. *Georgina is gone.*

37

SUSANNA rolls over, groggy, facing:

TOBIAS JACOBS – NAKED ON THE MATTRESS BESIDE HER.

WE ARE: INT. TOBIAS'S APARTMENT – NIGHT (FLASHBACK)

An ashtray of Gauloise butts. SUSANNA is also naked, on her back, smoking. A spark in her eye – she trusts this guy.

> TOBIAS
> I mean – everybody thinks about it –
> – *at some point.*

> SUSANNA
> How would you do it?

> TOBIAS
> I don't know.
> (beat)
> I guess I *haven't* really thought about it.

> SUSANNA
> Cut your wrists in the tub? Gun in the mouth? Hang from the rafters?

> TOBIAS
> Sometimes I imagine I just disappear.

> SUSANNA
> That's good. Vague but good.

Tobias smiles – he's getting uncomfortable with death talk. However, Susanna's just getting going – *she loves it.*

> Once it's in your head, though, you become *tainted.* You become a strange new breed. A life-form which enjoys fantasizing about its own demise. Perverse? Perhaps. But now, you can't stop thinking about it. Anything becomes part of the debate. Make a stupid remark? Kill yourself. Like the movie? You'll live. Miss the train? Kill yourself.

> TOBIAS
> I don't want to talk about this anymore.

Susanna turns. Confused. She was having fun.

SUSANNA

Why not?

TOBIAS

'Cause it's stupid.

Susanna pulls away, as if struck. Jumps up and dresses.

What?! 'Cause I don't want to die – that's not cool to you?

SUSANNA

I don't want to die –
I was just talking. *Jesus.*

Tobias sits up, sensing everything is ruined, getting angry.

TOBIAS

The world is fucked up, okay?
I'm down with that.

Susanna rolls her eyes, pulling on her jeans in a hurry.

It's so fucked up – *even though I dig living in it* – if some draft
zombie pulls my birthday out of a barrel, *I'm gonna die.*

Susanna buttons up her blouse, unimpressed.

SUSANNA

When's your birthday?

TOBIAS

June twenty-ninth.

Susanna grabs her bag, heading for the door.

SUSANNA

I'll pray for you.

SHE OPENS THE DOOR AND REVEALS:

LILLIAN THE NURSE, HOLDING A CLIPBOARD.

LILLIAN

Checks.

WE ARE BACK IN SUSANNA'S ROOM AT CLAYMOORE.

39

SUSANNA OPENS HER EYES: looking at the crumpled pillow beside her head.

CUT TO:

WATER BUBBLES AND STEAMS

SUSANNA lies in A HUGE TUB, staring at the ceiling. We are in a GREEN-TILED HYDROTHERAPY ROOM. *Water drips from hoses.* Chrome plate stimulation devices encircle the tubs.

ONE OF THE CATATONICS SITS IN AN ADJACENT BATH. Unmoving, a string of drool running from her lip.

THE DOOR OPENS – VALERIE ROUNDS THE TILED CORNER. She holds out a razor. Susanna takes it and waits for Valerie to exit, but VALERIE SITS ON A STOOL WITH A PAPERBACK.

SUSANNA

Are you going to watch?

VALERIE

'Fraid so. I guess that's why there's so many hairy legs around here.

Susanna sighs. She begins to shave her calf.

SUSANNA

'Anybody ever watch *you* shave?

VALERIE

I got two kids and one bathroom. What do you think?

SUSANNA

I think you should lock the door.

VALERIE

Sometimes, I do.

Susanna nods and begins to shave her other leg. Valerie watches her, peering over her reading glasses. There's a tenderness in Susanna that Valerie finds endearing.

It'll get better, you know.

Susanna looks up. Valerie smiles and looks back to her book.
Susanna smiles to herself. She likes this woman.

CUT TO:

INT. SOUTH BELL – TV ROOM – DAY

CLOSE ON: SUSANNA'S JOURNAL AS SHE SCRAWLS THE WORDS:

TWO KIDS AND ONE BATHROOM

SUSANNA sits on the couch, writing, next to THE CATATONICS. She
puffs on her Gauloise.

ON TV A DRAFT LOTTERY IN PROGRESS: *SEVERAL SELECTIVE
SERVICE BOARD MEMBERS watch capsules tumbling in a wire drum.*

MARGIE (THE JUNIOR NURSE) READS THE PAPER.

JANET and M-G sit on the opposite couch.
M-G is drugged, mouth open. She giggles at the Draft Lottery:

                    M-G
    Bingo. It's bingo.

                    JANET
    Stakes are higher, M-G.

*ON-SCREEN: Advisory Board Members take turns pulling capsules,
posting them on a board. The dates roll across the TV screen. October
1st . . . June 29th.*

                    SUSANNA
    – Oh my God – June twenty-ninth. A guy I know was just
    drafted.

                    JANET
    What's his name?

                    SUSANNA
    – Toby.

                    JANET
    Well, he's dead now.

Janet stands and crosses to the window – *as we hear:*

41

DAISY

Get out! My room is FUCKING PRIVATE!

DOWN THE HALL – LISA HOVERS IN DAISY'S DOORWAY. ALL
HEADS TURN THEIR WAY. Including Susanna.

LISA

I'm not *in* your room, Daisy-Mae! Look. I'm right fuckin'
here.
(holding out some nail polish)
I was just gonna offer you some of my –

SLAM! DAISY'S DOOR SLAMS SHUT IN LISA'S FACE.
Lisa stands there a beat, then turns, recovering instantly, blowing
on her nails. Unlike last night, Lisa is lucid, her movements brisk.
She sashays past Margie *her eyes are riveted on Susanna,* who
stiffens, closing her journal.

MARGIE

You're looking better, Lisa.

LISA

Why thanks, Margie – how's that engagement going?

MARGIE

Oh, *you know* –

LISA

No – I don't. I've been away.

MARGIE

– Joe wants me to – before the wedding.

LISA

Fuck his brains out – use a rubber.

MARGIE
(laughs)
Oh, gosh. I don't know.

LISA parks herself on the arm of the couch *BESIDE SUSANNA.*

LISA

Can I bum?

42

SUSANNA

Excuse me?

LISA

Can – I – bum – one?

Susanna nods coolly to the pack on the coffee table.

SUSANNA

Go ahead.

Lisa takes a cigarette and crosses, leaning over Margie, who lights it without looking up from her paper. Lisa moves to the opposite side of the couch beside a Catatonic. Kicks up her heels, strums her nails.

Susanna watches as Lisa blows a cloud of smoke at one of the Catatonics. There is no reaction. Lisa smiles at Susanna.

LISA

'Had your first Melvin yet?

SUSANNA
(turns, wary)

Who's Melvin?

LISA

Bald guy with a little pecker and a fat wife.

Margie chuckles from behind her paper.

– Your th-*rapist*, sweet pea. Unless they're giving you shocks or, God forbid, letting you out. Then, you see the great and wonderful Dr Dyke.

MARGIE

She means Dr Wick.

SUSANNA

I was in his office – but I didn't see him.

MARTIAN'S GIRLFRIEND
He's a she! Wick is a girl!

LISA

That's right, M-G. Wick is a chick.

> (grins at Susanna)

Hence the nickname.

> (to Lillian – passing)

Hey, Lil. When the fuck is my check-up?

LILLIAN

Now – it's *now*, Lisa. You said you'd be in your room.

> (down the hall)

John, she's here!

The phone rings.

Margie crosses into the nurse's station to answer it.

MARGIE

Susanna. You've got Melvin in a half-hour. I'll take you there.

Lisa struts off with Lillian, looking back at Susanna.

LISA

'Can't let you sit too long without popping the hood.

Suddenly alone except for the Catatonics and M-G, SUSANNA sits back and stares bitterly at:

THE TELEVISION. *More draft dates travel across the screen.*

Susanna turns, glaring at THE NEAREST CATATONIC.
She blows a cloud of smoke at her. THE WOMAN TURNS. ANGRY.

CATATONIC

Asshole.

SUSANNA IS STUNNED.

MARGIE

Susanna. *Phone call. Booth one.*

> CUT TO:

INT. SOUTH BELL – HALLWAY PHONES – DAY

SUSANNA picks up a phone. It's dead.

SUSANNA

Hello?

VALERIE struts by, exchanging words with DR CORNISH who heads down the stairs. Valerie smiles at Susanna and crosses into the Nurse's station. Susanna tries the next phone.

Hello?

ANNETTE
(off-screen)

Susanna?

SUSANNA

Hi, Mom.

ANNETTE
(off-screen)
Your father's on, too. He just got back from the Reserve hearings. His plane got stuck at Dulles.

CARL
(off-screen)
How are you doing, honey?

SUSANNA

I'm fine, Dad.

Susanna watches as DAISY THROWS A FIT DIRECTED AT MARGIE THROUGH THE DUTCH DOORS OF THE DISPENSARY.

DAISY
How come that *sociopath* gets *nail polish,* but I can't get something *medical* to help me *function?*

ANNETTE
(off-screen)
We talked to your nurse this morning – you were still asleep. She said you were well.

MARGIE
No more, Daisy. That's what Dr Cornish put on your chart.

CARL
(off-screen)
A black lady, I take it. Crumble said it was progressive there. Like a resort hotel.

SUSANNA

Yeah. It's nice.

45

MEANWHILE, DAISY CONFRONTS VALERIE AT THE NURSE'S
STATION:

> DAISY
> *Valerie!* Please. If you
> can't give me Ex-Lax
> then give me some
> Colace!

> ANNETTE
> (off-screen)
> Have you made any new
> friends?

> VALERIE
> *No!* They said no
> more laxatives.

> SUSANNA
> Mom. This isn't Camp
> Winetka.

> MARGIE
> I can get her some prune juice.

SCREAMING, DAISY storms toward her room, past SUSANNA.

> DAISY
> *This is outrageous!*

As Daisy marches towards her room, she and Susanna exchange A
BRIEF GLANCE. Daisy SLAMS her door – *NO TRESPASSING*.

> ANNETTE
> (off-screen)
> . . . Susanna – I'm sorry I didn't take you myself, but Dr
> Crumble said it would be better if –
> > (weeping)
> – I *wanted to.*

> SUSANNA
> Mom. It's okay. Hey. If they met the whole family, maybe
> we'd all 'been committed'.

> CARL
> (off-screen)
> That's uncalled-for, young lady.

Susanna can hear her mom, still crying. She hangs up the phone.

> CUT TO:

INT. MELVIN'S OFFICE – DAY

A DESKPLATE READS: MELVIN BUNDT, MD.

TILT UP TO – CLOSE ON: Melvin, a soft-spoken man in his forties. There is a picture of his wife (rotund) and his child (rotund) on his desk. He smokes.

SUSANNA sits in an armchair, also smoking.

> MELVIN
> Why are you using the past tense?

> SUSANNA
> What do you mean?

> MELVIN
> He was only drafted today so, chances are, he's not dead yet. 'Probably has several months before he reports.

> SUSANNA
> *Whatever.* He was – he's just a nice guy. That's all. So I felt bad.

> MELVIN
> But you've been feeling bad in general, right? You've been depressed.

> SUSANNA
> I haven't been a ball of joy, Melvin.

> MELVIN
> I understand you tried to kill yourself last week. Is there anything you want to tell me about that?

> SUSANNA
> I had a headache.

> MELVIN
> So I assume you took the recommended aspirin dosage for a headache.

Susanna adjusts – *a worthy opponent.*

> SUSANNA
> I didn't try to kill myself.

MELVIN

What were you trying to do?

SUSANNA

I was trying to make the shit stop.

MELVIN
(reading her file)
The time jumps, the depression, the headaches, the thing with your hand –

SUSANNA

All of the above.

MELVIN

I see.

SUSANNA

You people always say 'I see' when clearly you don't.

Susanna looks out the window.

MELVIN

What were your other experiences with therapy like?

On the lawn, A NAKED MALE PATIENT streaks past, through the leaves. He is gone as quickly as he appeared and Susanna is left wondering whether she even saw him.

SUSANNA

Are my parents coming here?

MELVIN

– Do you miss them?

She shakes her head.

– I'm going to suggest they give you a few weeks. To settle in.

Susanna nods. The cigarette trembles in her fingers.

SUSANNA

They're gonna love this.

A sadness overtakes Susanna – looking outside:

On the lawn ORDERLIES RESTRAIN THE PRANCING MAN.

48

MELVIN
You seem puzzled about something.

Susanna quietly cries, her eyes unmoving from the window.

SUSANNA
Well, Melvin, I'm puzzled about why it is I have to be in a
mental institution.

MELVIN
You put yourself here, Susanna.

SUSANNA
My *parents* put me here.

MELVIN
No, they didn't.

Hot tears run down Susanna's cheeks.

SUSANNA
Everyone here is fucking *crazy!*

MELVIN
So, you want to go home.

Susanna turns, eyes red.

SUSANNA
Same problem.

CUT TO:

INT. SOUTH BELL — TV ROOM — AFTERNOON

SUSANNA WATCHES AS LISA TAKES HER MEDS.
Slung upside-down on a couch, Lisa takes a pill cup from GRETTA
and routinely swallows, her eyes down the hall.

SUSANNA TURNS FOLLOWING LISA'S GAZE:

DOWN THE HALL: DAISY KISSES HER FATHER GOODBYE.
A potato-faced man, he hands her TWO FOIL-WRAPPED
CHICKENS. He departs, nods to Valerie.

SUSANNA turns back, meeting eyes with LISA, upside-down. Lisa

49

smiles and SPITS HER PILLS INTO HER PALM. She discreetly displays them to Susanna – then slips them in her pocket.

> GRETTA
> (off-screen)

Susanna.

Gretta stands before Susanna, holding A CUP WITH TWO PINK PILLS.

> SUSANNA

What are these?

> GRETTA

Colace. A laxative.

> SUSANNA

I don't need them.

> GRETTA

Are we going to have a problem?

Susanna looks to Lisa – puts the pills in her mouth.

> CUT TO:

INT. SOUTH BELL – OUTSIDE DAISY'S DOOR – DAY

NO TRESPASSING says the sign on Daisy's door. SUSANNA knocks. *Lisa watches her from the lobby.*

> SUSANNA

Daisy.

> DAISY

Fuck off.

> SUSANNA

I got something you want.

THE DOOR FLINGS OPEN. Susanna enters, looking back as – IN THE LOBBY – LISA WATCHES, *STUNNED.*

> CUT TO:

INT. DAISY'S ROOM – DAY

A FOIL-WRAPPED CHICKEN sits open on the floral bedspread.
DAISY sits on the bed, pulling meat away in strips.

SUSANNA stands in the room. Daisy offers no response, lining up
chicken strips on the foil, like a Japanese chef. Susanna sits down.
She watches Daisy – *waiting*.

> SUSANNA
> – I saw a guy once on the subway – and he was all wrapped
> up in tin foil.

Daisy pays no attention. Susanna notices clothes stacked neatly in
A SUITCASE. *Ready to move at a moment's notice.*

> Why are you all packed up?

> DAISY
> I'm out of here in a month. My dad got me an apartment.

> SUSANNA
> Where? What kind of apartment?

> DAISY
> Near the airport. One bedroom, two baths, eat-in chicken. He
> fixed it up for me.

> SUSANNA
> – you mean, eat-in kitchen.

> DAISY
> That's what I said, asshole.
>   (looking up, impatient)
> So, what do you got that I want?

Susanna opens her hand.

IN HER PALM: THE TWO PINK LAXATIVE PILLS.

> Put 'em on the bed and get out.

> LISA
>   (off-screen)
> Put *yours* on the bed.

LISA STANDS IN THE OPEN DOORWAY.

> DAISY

Oh, Jesus. *Get out.*

> LISA

Don't take advantage, Daise – just 'cause she's new. Pony up some Valium.

> DAISY

Get the fuck out or I'm calling Valerie.

> LISA

Go ahead. Ask Val for some Colace – like Susie Q's got *in her fucking hand.*
>> (aside)

Why does it stink in here?

> DAISY

I don't take Valium.

> LISA

That's the point, Daise. They give them to you – *and you don't take them.*
>> (stepping into the room)

What are you making with that chicken?
'You gonna eat that?

Swish: GRETTA PEERS IN THE DOOR.

> GRETTA

Checks.
>> (beat, smiles)

Hey. You've got visitors, Daisy!

> LISA

Mark it in the book, Gretta. Daisy's going social.

> DAISY
>> (to Gretta)

I want some fucking Colace.

> GRETTA
>> (smiles, departing)

Talk to Melvin tomorrow.

LISA PUSHES THE DOOR CLOSED. *Ka-clunk.*

> **LISA**
> I think you want to poop, Daisy. I think it's been days.

Susanna stands. Offers the pills to Daisy.

> **SUSANNA**
> Look. It's okay. I don't care.

> **LISA**
> But I *do*. I do care. *Sit down!*

Susanna sits. Lisa moves about the room, plays with Daisy's porcelain figurines. Finds postcards stacked on the dresser.

> Daddy buys you a private. No one gets in. You leave only when Valerie makes you go to the cafeteria – *where you never eat.* You're a laxative junkie, so I figure you're like Janet, but then, here you are with this chicken. *What's with that?*

> **DAISY**
> My dad owns a deli, *asshole* – with a rotisserie. I like my dad's chicken. When I eat something else – I puke.

LISA EXAMINES THE POSTCARDS IN HER HAND. She reads them: *From Hawaii, Florida, Italy, there is a sickly sweetness to the inscriptions, each ending with: love and kisses. Daddy.*

> **SUSANNA**
> So, your dad brings you your favorite food every week.

Daisy nods.

> **LISA**
> How does he know you're eating it?

> **DAISY**
> *He knows.*

> **LISA**
> What about the bones? Doesn't Valerie –

> **DAISY**
> Unlike you two, I'm not interested in killing myself.

Lisa notices SOME FOIL PEEKING OUT FROM UNDER THE BED.

SUSANNA

Why can't you eat in the cafeteria?

DAISY

What do you like better, taking a dump alone or with Valerie watching?

SUSANNA

– alone –

DAISY

Everyone likes to be alone when it comes out – I like to be alone when it goes in. To me, the cafeteria is like being with twenty girls at once all taking a dump.

LISA
(laughing)

Daisy. That's fucked up.

DAISY

Show me the cat on your arm. Show me *Ruby* – and we have a deal.

LISA

No.

DAISY

Why not?

LISA

Because I'm bored and I want to go.
(exiting, to Susanna)
Come on. *Come on!*

Daisy retrieves TWO VALIUM FROM A RAGGEDY ANN'S HEAD. SHE THROWS THEM ON THE BED.

DAISY

Alright, asshole. *Alright!*

SUSANNA DROPS HER PILLS ON THE BED AND DAISY *INHALES THEM.* LISA SCOOPS UP THE VALIUM, swallows them, *and* suddenly – LEAPS TO THE FLOOR, LOOKING UNDER DAISY'S BED.

Hey!

SEVEN FOIL-WRAPPED CHICKEN CARCASSES LIE ON THE FLOOR.
Arranged chronologically: on the right the oldest, mold-encrusted;
to the left, fresh carcasses.

> LISA
> (holding her nose, gagging)
> Dios fucking mio.

Susanna kneels beside Lisa, staring at the carcasses.

> *'how Daddy knows she's eating.*

> DAISY
> When I get ten, Valerie makes me throw them away.

SUSANNA AND LISA look at one another in disbelief.

CUT TO:

INT. SUSANNA'S ROOM — NIGHT

CLOSE ON: SUSANNA'S JOURNAL AS SHE SCRAWLS THE WORDS:

IF YOU LIVED HERE, YOU'D BE HOME NOW.

SUSANNA looks up to see LISA sitting on the end of her bed.

> LISA
> Scribble, scribble, scribble.
> *Written anything about me yet?*

GEORGINA looks up from her book, half asleep. Her little radio
plays. SUSANNA closes her journal, tight. Lisa grins.

> SUSANNA
> Don't do that.

> LISA
> Do what?

> SUSANNA
> Scare me.

> LISA
> (smiles gently)
> Okay.

55

SUSANNA

I get scared at night. That's all.

LISA

Of what? Of what are you scared?

SUSANNA

Nothing. This thing – nevermind.

GEORGINA

Lisa – is Daisy really getting out?

LISA
(nods)

She coughed up a big one.

SUSANNA

But she's crazy.

LISA
(smiles)

Hey, man. That's what th-*rape*-me's all about. Why do you
think Freud's picture is on every shrink's wall? He created a
fucking industry. *Lie down – confess your secret – you're saved –
ka-ching!* The more you confess, the more they think about
setting you free.

Susanna takes this in, disturbed.

SUSANNA

What if you don't have a secret?

LISA

Then, you're a lifer – like me.

GEORGINA

You're a lifer because you keep *coming back*!
(to Susanna)
She's escaped nine times and she keeps coming back.

LISA

Liar.
(back to Susanna)
Six times. I've been out *six* times in twelve years.

56

SUSANNA
So, why do you come back?

LISA
You ever watch that TV? It's a mess out there, baby.
Here – *shit* – they feed me, they do my laundry, fresh sheets,
buy me cigarettes.
(smiles)
Mom and Pop ain't gonna put me up at the Hilton.

CUT TO:

INT. MELVIN'S OFFICE – DAY

SUSANNA stares out the window, holding a carton of Gauloise.
CARL AND ANNETTE – beside her, anxious, out of their element.

ANNETTE
I was changing her diaper – and I turned to get the powder –
and while my back was turned, she *rolled off the bed* – rolled off
and broke her leg. The doctor put her in a body cast, but he
also strapped her down. They do that with babies –

CARL
Annette! This has nothing to do with –

SUSANNA
(stunned)
You never told me this!

ANNETTE
Carl had been planning this trip – to Santa Monica. We
couldn't postpone it – he had a commitment at RAND – so
we took her with us – strapped to *this board* – on the back seat
– four thousand miles.

MELVIN
If you like, Mrs Kaysen – we can discuss that further on the
way out, but I doubt –

CARL
Just how long is she going to be here?

MELVIN

With all due respect, Mr Kaysen, psychiatry and economics are a bit different. The length of Susanna's stay isn't fixed – it depends on her response to *treatment*.

CARL

Treatment for *what*? Depression? Look. Mr Bundt, *before* I was an economist –

MELVIN

Susanna tells me you were an advisor to President Kennedy –

CARL

– before *that* – I was a *teacher*. I taught people her age. That was my job. And I can tell you, *they're all depressed*.

ANNETTE

She's always been shy.

Melvin's eyes fall on Susanna. An uncomfortable pause.

CARL

It's almost Christmas. What are we supposed to tell the people who care about her?

SUSANNA

What you don't understand, Melvin, is that my parents are having a holiday cocktail party crisis.

CARL

Sus*anna*!

ANNETTE

What exactly is the *borderline* business you mentioned on the phone?

On the word 'borderline', Susanna looks up.

MELVIN

Look. This information is not useful – to Susanna – it's not useful – not *now*.

SUSANNA

What borderline business?

MELVIN

The mind is the only organ where *awareness* of its condition can *affect* its recovery.

SUSANNA

What borderline?! Borderline between what and what? *Melvin!*

MELVIN

It's a condition, Susanna – known as *Borderline Personality Disorder.*

Annette immediately begins to cry. Loud.

It's not uncommon. Especially among young women.

ANNETTE

– what causes it?

MELVIN

We're not sure.

SUSANNA

Is it genetic?

CARL

Oh, *Christ*, Susanna.

MELVIN

It *is* five times more common among those with a borderline parent.

Carl and Annette become ashen – *they're ready to leave.*

CUT TO:

INT. TV ROOM – DAY – LATER

SUSANNA STANDS AT THE WINDOW, WATCHING –

HER PARENTS TRUDGING TO THEIR VOLVO – WITH MELVIN.

CYNTHIA, LISA and POLLY are playing cards at a table.
JOHN pushes a cart down the hall, his eyes dart to Susanna.

JOHN

Hey, Susanna.

Susanna turns. He's sweet. She smiles.

CYNTHIA

John, will you call me a cab?

JOHN

Okay, you're a cab.

Cynthia laughs hysterically as John exits.

SUSANNA watches her parents pull away. She feels LISA WATCHING HER. She meets Lisa's eyes. Lisa smiles coy, and looks away, arranging her cards.

LISA

Razors pain you. Rivers are damp.
Acid stains you. Drugs cause cramp.
Guns aren't lawful. Nooses give.
Gas smells awful. You might as well live.
                    (slapping down her cards)
Gin. I'm gone.

Lisa crosses past JANET and the TWO CATATONICS watching a movie on television. She snaps it off, moving down the hall.

JANET

Asshole!

Janet turns the TV back on. The tube comes to life.

SUSANNA'S EYES move to the TV – she sits down.
Fred Astaire, dances on the ceiling. Polly starts to dance about the room to the music. Janet turns to Susanna.

Lisa says you got into Daisy's room.
'Said it was filled with chickens.

Susanna nods. Lillian calls out from the nurses' station.

LILLIAN

Susanna. You have a phone call.

CUT TO:

INT. PHONE BOOTH – HALLWAY – DAY

SUSANNA picks up the phone in the first booth. Apprehensive.

> VOICE
> So. What's your diag-nonsense?

> SUSANNA
> *Who is this?*

> VOICE
> What'd he say to Mom and Pop?
> What's your *malady*?

SUSANNA TURNS TO SEE: LISA TWO BOOTHS DOWN, ON THE PHONE:

> SUSANNA
> I have a borderline personality.

> LISA
> That's like – *nothing*. What else?

> SUSANNA
> He didn't want to say more –
> He said it would affect my recovery.

> LISA
> Tongue your meds tonight. After one o'clock checks, Gretta goes out for a smoke. Check in the mirrors, if you're clear, go to Hector's closet – by the art room. It'll be open.

Lisa hangs up and walks off. *Susanna watches her.*

CUT TO:

INT. SUSANNA AND GEORGINA'S ROOM – NIGHT

Under the blankets, SUSANNA pulls on her jeans.
GEORGINA sleeps in the background. The clock says one.

Click, swish. LILLIAN peers in.

SUSANNA FREEZES – FEIGNS SLEEP.

CUT TO:

INT. HECTOR'S SUPPLY CLOSET/HALL – NIGHT

Glancing at a security mirror to see that it's clear, SUSANNA SCAMPERS DOWN THE HALL. She opens the door. Enters quickly. She stands there in the dark closet, feeling stupid. Suddenly, in the shadows, she notices –

TWO GLISTENING BLUE EYES. Silent. Quiet.

> POLLY
> *– you're beautiful –*

Crouched in the shadows, POLLY watches Susanna with utter admiration. She reaches – touching Susanna's cheek. Beat.

> SUSANNA
> Did you really set yourself on fire because of your puppy?

> POLLY
> Who told you that?

> SUSANNA
> Georgina.

> POLLY
> Do you believe her?

> SUSANNA
> She's a pathological liar.

> POLLY
> (smiles)
> Only to authority figures.

SUDDENLY, THE DOOR OPENS. *IT'S LISA. HOLDING A KEY-RING.*

> CUT TO:

INT. ART ROOM – NIGHT

M-G, CYNTHIA, JANET, LISA AND SUSANNA shuffle to the side exit where Lisa reveals A DIVOT OF ART CLAY WHICH SHE STUCK IN THE LOCK, KEEPING THE DOOR OPEN. THEY FILE DOWN THE STAIRS EXCEPT Polly, who lingers, staring at –

THE LOCKED CAGE ADORNED WITH MUSICAL INSTRUMENTS:

> LISA

Polly!

Polly joins them on the stairs – she whispers to Susanna:

> POLLY
> Some musician gave 'em to the hospital after they cured him
> – of his addiction. But they keep 'em locked up since Becky
> Martin slit her wrists with an E-string.

> CUT TO:

INT. BASEMENT – NIGHT

KaCHUNK. A DOOR OPENS ON TO: A NETWORK OF TUNNELS.
LISA, CYNTHIA, M-G, POLLY, SUSANNA AND JANET HEAD into the
tunnel, around a blind corner. There the tunnel bisects; one part
leading to a staircase up, the other *INTO A DARKER TUNNEL.*

> CUT TO:

WALKING IN THE PITCH-BLACK TUNNELS – NIGHT

Footsteps on wet cement. Pipes everywhere. Susanna looks about,
wide-eyed. Suddenly – *FLUTTER, FLUTTER, FLUTTER.*

> POLLY

What was that?

> SUSANNA

Probably a bat.

> JANET

It wasn't a blue jay.

> POLLY
> Around this corner – it'll be light.

Faint light emanates from the end of the tunnel. Flashlights are
turned off. Walls glisten with moisture.

> JANET
> When they built this place they put tunnels in so the loons
> didn't have to go anywhere in the cold.

SUSANNA

I missed that in the brochure.

POLLY

Now they dunk us in freezing water.

They pass another junction in the tunnel.

LISA

Watch it, there's a dip.

Susanna side-steps A RECESSED AREA in the floor that's wet. She veers to the left. Lisa grabs her.

POLLY

– that goes to the sheds. Lisa's *way out.*

Susanna looks to Lisa. Lisa raises her brow. Grins.

LISA

Some other time, Susie-Q.

CUT TO:

ANOTHER TUNNEL. DRIPPING PIPES

THE GIRLS ARE HUDDLED AROUND A DOOR FRAMED IN THE WALL. Cynthia uses a bobby-pin to pick the lock.

We're under administration.
(jingles her keys)
No good here.

JANET

Thank God this place has a sliding scale – we get to comingle with lock-pickin' trash.

Cynthia smiles – thinks it's a compliment.

Click – THE DOOR OPENS A FEW INCHES – CHAINED FROM THE OTHER SIDE. SKINNY JANET SLIDES THROUGH – INTO A DARK CHAMBER. She unchains the door from the other side. IT OPENS.

Fluorescents sputter on. Susanna stares at:

64

A DUSTY REGULATION SIZE SINGLE-LANE BOWLING ALLEY

THERE ARE TWO BOWLING BALLS – heavy, with huge finger holes. M-G grabs one. Slings it down the alley into the gutter.

JANET trudges to the pin-pit, a lit cig on her lip. She retrieves M-G's ball, puts it in the return chute. LISA lights a cigarette.

> JANET
>
> Alright, you're up.

> SUSANNA
>
> *Me?* I don't know – I only did this once in my life.

> LISA
>
> Shut up and bowl, woman.

Susanna stands at the lane, struggling with the heavy ball. She feels all eyes on her. She drops the ball. *THUD*. It meanders down the lane, really slow – but straight –

Everyone watches, slack-jawed AS SUSANNA'S BALL LETHARGICALLY TAKES OUT EVERY SINGLE PIN. *A CHEER.*

Susanna smiles, red-faced, as the motley crew applauds and whoops. *The first friends she's had in years.* She sits down on a bench next to Lisa as:

CYNTHIA steps on to the lane with a big red ball. She does a little two-step then lets loose – powerfully. HER BALL SLAMS INTO THE PINS – *a few left standing*. Janet and M-G argue about how to keep score. Susanna and Lisa sit and watch like mothers on a park bench.

> SUSANNA
>
> Georgina's *right on.*

> LISA
>
> About what?

Susanna points to each of the girls, in *sing-song*:

> SUSANNA
> (to M-G)
>
> 'if I only had a *brain* –

(to Polly)

– *a face.*

(to Janet)

– *some hips.*

(to Cynthia)

– *a dick.*

Lisa smiles as Janet swings a big ball and it flies backward from her hand, bouncing to the wall. *All the girls laugh.*

CUT TO:

INT. CONFERENCE ROOM – WICK'S OFFICE – NIGHT

POLLY CLIMBS FROM A DUMB WAITER, JOINING LISA, CYNTHIA, JANET AND SUSANNA. THEY ENTER DR WICK'S OFFICE.

Suddenly – VRRRRRMMMMMMM. *Silence broken by a ROARING MOTOR.* M-G STRUGGLES WITH A VACUUM. It runs away from her, spinning.

JANET

Mother of God. *Turn it off!*

M-G

I can't!

LISA

Hold this.

Lisa passes the flashlight to Susanna – AND JERKS THE POWER PLUG FROM THE WALL. The beast is quiet. Lisa turns, calmly facing M-G and – SMACKS HER ACROSS THE FACE. M-G crumples into a ball.

THE GIRLS SCRAMBLE INTO WICK'S OFFICE – BUT SUSANNA LINGERS – watching as Lisa strokes M-G's hair. M-G cries.

CUT TO:

CLOSE ON: A FILE. THE NAME: *KAYSEN, S.*

FINGERS FLIP THROUGH SUSANNA'S FILE – PSYCHIATRIC REPORTS – the word BORDERLINE seems to jump out. Among other words such as RESISTANT, DENIAL, HIGHLY INTELLIGENT, DEPRESSIVE.

CLOSE ON: SUSANNA'S EYES, RIVETED.

In the corner, M-G pouts in the corner, red-eyed.

WIDER: THE FILE DRAWERS ARE THROWN OPEN. THE GIRLS SIT ALL AROUND THE OFFICE, READING. LISA sits on the file cabinet, foraging her file. Her eyes scan SOMETHING UPSETTING.

> LISA

Fuck you, Melvin.

> JANET

Want to see mine? *Then let me see yours.*

LISA AND JANET TRADE FILES. Janet reads aloud:

> *'Highs and lows increasingly severe.*
> *Controlling relationships with patients.'*

SUSANNA LOOKS UP.

> *'No appreciable response to meds.*
> *No remission observed.'*
> (looking up)
> And that was *before* you ran away.

In the corner, POLLY SITS WITH HER FILE ON HER LAP. The others converse in the background as POLLY READS – painfully.

> LISA

We are very rare. And mostly we are men.

> JANET

Lisa thinks she's hot shit because she's a sociopath.

> CYNTHIA

I'm a sociopath.

> LISA

No. You're a dyke.

CLOSE ON: POLLY'S FILE.

THE WORDS: severe avoidance disorder. Suicidal. Refuses to acknowledge disfigurement.

POLLY'S EYES become wet with sadness. She flips past the evaluations and comes upon A SCHOOL PICTURE OF HERSELF. BLUE EYES. SO YOUNG. SMILING. UN-SCARRED. Tears drop on to the photograph. POLLY CLOSES THE FILE. *Weeping.*

M-G, in the opposite corner, smiles at Polly, comforting.

Susanna crosses, reading from A MANUAL OF MENTAL DISORDERS.

> SUSANNA
> 'Borderline personality'. An instability of self-image, relationships and mood. Uncertainty about goals. Impulsive in activities that are self-damaging, such as casual sex' . . .

> LISA
> *I like that.*

> SUSANNA
> 'Social contrariness and a generally pessimistic attitude are often observed.' *That's me, alright.*

> LISA
> That's everybody.

> SUSANNA
> What sex isn't casual?

> JANET
> They mean promiscuous.

> SUSANNA
> I'm not promiscuous.
> (off Lisa's look)
> *I'm not!*

> LISA
> What's your count?

> SUSANNA
> It depends – on what all is in the count.

LISA

Everything from fooling around with clothes on to dry
humping to hand jobs through blow jobs to straight fucking.

SUDDENLY: *bong, bong, bong, bong.*
ALL THE GIRLS GASP – SPINNING AROUND.

IN THE CORNER – *A GRANDFATHER CLOCK STRIKES FOUR. LOUD.*

A COLLECTIVE SIGH. Lisa looks to Susanna.
SUDDENLY – *THE SOUND OF A KEY TURNING A LOCK.*
The door to the outer office opens and –

A HUGE BEAM OF LIGHT from a hand-held security searchlight
slices into the inner office. *AN OLD SECURITY GUARD.*

THE GIRLS SCRAMBLE ON ALL FOURS, crawling behind the desk,
into the closet, behind the door – *any cover they can find.*

SUSANNA CROUCHES, BEHIND THE FILE CABINET. HER HANDS
PRESSED AGAINST *AGING FLORAL WALLPAPER.*
THE OLD SECURITY GUARD shuffles into Wick's office. His bright
light flits at his side, making shifting shadows as he crosses to
Wick's desk, standing right above –

LISA, JANET AND POLLY. They hold their breath, his hands
fumbling inches away as he reaches into THE BOTTOM DRAWER.
He retrieves A BOTTLE OF VODKA AND A GLASS.

He pours a shot and sits in a squeaky swivel chair. He leafs
through a *Life* magazine, the chair squeaking rhythmically. POLLY
is pinned closest to him, terrified, her blue eyes looking straight
out at A PAGE OF MARILYN MONROE PHOTOS, draped on the
guard's lap. *His chair squeaks, like a mattress.*

SUSANNA, PALMS ON THE WALL, STARES AT THE CRACKED
WALLPAPER. *The squeaking continues. Her eyes follow a crack as it
swoops downward and then up again, making the shape of the state of –*

SUSANNA

. . . *Florida.*

The squeaking stops.

PROFESSOR GILCREST
(off-screen)
What? Why did you stop?

SUSANNA IS FROZEN, NAKED, HANDS ON THE WALL, SITTING
ATOP – PROFESSOR GILCREST, SWEATY, RED-FACED ON A
LEATHER COUCH.

WE ARE: INT. COLLEGE OFFICE – NIGHT (FLASHBACK)

She runs her finger over the crack, looking down to him.

SUSANNA
The crack in the wall – it looks like –

PROFESSOR GILCREST
Susanna. You're not into some weird bondage bag, are you?

No answer. Gilcrest stares up at:

– *your wrist.*

The inside of Susanna's wrist is black and blue.

A flare of light and the sound of a drawer slamming closed.

WE ARE: BACK IN WICK'S OFFICE – NIGHT

THE SECURITY GUARD shuffles out of the door.

THE GIRLS – SWEATY – ALL CLIMB OUT OF THEIR HIDING
PLACES.

POLLY
That was forever and a day.

LISA looks to SUSANNA, dazed.

SUSANNA
How long was he in here?

Lisa is disturbed by this question. Janet turns.

Tick, tock, tick, tock. Susanna turns to –

THE GRANDFATHER CLOCK IN THE CORNER – *it is four twenty-five.*

CUT TO:

EXT. SOUTH BELL – WALKING TO THE ROAD – DAY

Ka-kunch, ka-kunch, ka-kunch. Rubber boots bustling through crusted snow.

SUSANNA, LISA, GEORGINA, POLLY, M-G AND CYNTHIA WALK IN A PACK, enjoying the crunch, crunch of their boots.

VALERIE, DAISY, AND THE STUDENT NURSES (MARGIE, GRETTA) walk on the salted sidewalk. *They watch the girls.*

> SUSANNA
>
> *Jesus.*

Susanna stares ahead in wonder at JANET, WHO WALKS ALONE on the snow bank. She's so thin, she never breaks the crust.

> LISA
>
> Valerie's freaking out.

VALERIE SCOLDS M-G FOR JUMPING TOO MUCH.

DAISY EYES LISA AND SUSANNA.

Margie and Gretta also look about. Vigilant. Paranoid.

> SUSANNA
>
> Taking us for ice-cream in a blizzard – 'makes you wonder who're the real wack-jobs.

Polly barrels into the conversation:

> POLLY
>
> I think it's nice. It's nice to do something nice on Daisy's last day.

CUT TO:

EXT. MIDDLE OF TOWN – DAY

THE TOWN IS DECORATED FOR CHRISTMAS.

THE STUDENT NURSES AND VALERIE have distributed themselves all around THE GIRLS, herding them – into a tight pack.

It is a strange sight, this huddle of wide-eyed girls in matching boots, shuffling down the street, surrounded by starched-white nurses. People walk by, trying not to stare. Pressed together, Susanna glares at Margie. Margie giggles. Like all the student nurses, Margie is the same age as the girls. Without uniforms, *they'd all look the same.*

THEY CROSS THE STREET TOWARD ECKEL'S ICE-CREAM PARLOR.

                                                        CUT TO:

INT. ECKEL'S ICE-CREAM PARLOR – DAY

An old-fashioned parlor, dotted with SUBURBAN MATRONS. THE GIRLS are at the counter muttering about flavors. Nervous nurses cling like Velcro. A PIMPLY-FACED TEENAGER is behind the counter with a big button that says '*RONNY*'.

Susanna looks around the shop. Suddenly, she spots MRS GILCREST HAVING A SUNDAE WITH HER DAUGHTER BONNIE.

                         SUSANNA
    Oh, God.

Susanna hides behind Lisa. Margie addresses Ronny.

                         MARGIE
    We'll have ten cones.

                         JANET
    Nine.

                         DAISY
    Eight.

                         LISA
    'Guess they don't have gelato pollo.

                         GEORGINA
    I want peppermint stick.

72

POLLY

Me too.

DAISY

It's just called peppermint.

M-G

Peppermint dick.

DAISY

Honestly.

M-G

PEPPERMINT CLIT!

Everyone in the parlor turns and stares.

VALERIE

We'll have four peppermints.

SUSANNA

Five.

VALERIE

Five. *Lisa?*

Everyone looks to Lisa, who leans on the counter and smiles.

LISA

– *rrrrRRonny* –

RONNY

– yes –

LISA

'you got hot fudge?

RONNY

– yes –

LISA

Alright, then. I want a vanilla sundae, with hot fudge, sprinkles
– *rainbow, not chocolate* – whipped cream, jimmies, cherries
. . . *um* . . .

Everyone waits as Lisa rolls her tongue, thinking:

RONNY

– nuts? –

Everyone bursts out laughing.

CUT TO:

INT. ECKEL'S ICE-CREAM PARLOR – LATER

JANET, GEORGINA, SUSANNA AND LISA are eating in a booth.
Susanna glances at THE GILCRESTS, A FEW TABLES AWAY.

IN THE NEXT BOOTH DAISY answers eager questions, trying to
avoid looking at M-G who is eating with her mouth wide open:

DAISY
– Melvin wanted me in a halfway house. But my dad thought
I deserved a place of my own. It has an eat-in chicken and
brand new wicker and –

LISTENING TO THIS, LISA IS HUNCHED OVER HER SUNDAE,
seething. SUSANNA is in mid-lick on her cone when MRS GILCREST
and BONNIE appear at the booth. From her expression it's clear
that Mrs Gilcrest knows of Susanna and her husband.

MRS GILCREST
Susanna? Do you remember me?
(fire in her eyes)
You *must* remember me.

SUSANNA
– Hi, Mrs Gilcrest. Hey, Bonnie.
How's Radcliffe?

BONNIE
Wellesley. I'm enjoying it. It's strong in art. I'm going to the
Sorbonne this summer.

SUSANNA
Oh. That's great!

MRS GILCREST
(leaning close)
You know – I know *all* about you. And I hope you're put
away *for EVER.*

74

Susanna is stunned.

LISA

Is this the professor's wife?

MRS GILCREST

Oh. So – I guess you've told *everyone*.

JANET

What professor?

Susanna is mortified. Valerie turns, watching, concerned.

LISA

Lady – back off –

MRS GILCREST	BONNIE
Was I talking to you?	Mother. We have to go.

LISA

No – you were *spitting* on me!
Mellow fucking out!

MRS GILCREST

Don't tell me what to do!

LISA

So she gave your husband a rim job. B-F-D.
(looking Gilcrest over)
I'm sure he was *begging* for it. I heard it was like a god
damned *toothpick* anyway.

MRS GILCREST

HOW DARE YOU – !? *HOW DARE YOU?!*

MRS GILCREST WAGS HER FINGER IN LISA'S FACE, BUT *LISA
GRABS HER WRIST – FIRMLY.*

LISA

Some advice? Don't point your finger at crazy people.

MRS GILCREST	VALERIE
LET GO OF ME!	(standing)
	Hey! Hey!

BUT LISA DOES NOT LET GO. Janet cackles. Susanna turns to Mrs

75

Gilcrest and smiles a toothy 'crazy' smile. BONNIE backs away, unnerved by everything, especially POLLY'S STARE.

<table>
<tr><td>BONNIE</td><td>VALERIE</td></tr>
<tr><td>Mu-ther!</td><td>LISA – STOP IT!</td></tr>
</table>

MRS GILCREST
YOU'RE NOT CRAZY – *YOU'RE DRUG ADDICTS!*

GEORGINA
You're the drug addict, bitch! You were smoking hash right over there! I SAW YOU!

MRS GILCREST
LET – GO – OF – ME!

LISA
(a full-on rabid loon, like Foghorn Leghorn)
What I'm saying is – *what I'm saying is – we're FUCKING CRAZY!*

<table>
<tr><td>SUSANNA</td><td>JANET</td></tr>
<tr><td>*BLAHHHHHHH!*</td><td>(snapping, dog-like)
GRRRRR!</td></tr>
</table>

BONNIE
(tearful)
Moh-ther. *We have to go!*

BONNIE'S ICE-CREAM TOO CLOSE TO DAISY'S FACE – WHO SMACKS IT.

DAISY
Watch it, asshole!

LISA RELEASES MRS GILCREST AND THE GIRLS BEAT A RETREAT.

CUT TO:

EXT. APPROACHING SOUTH BELL – DAY

AS THEY ALL TRUDGE BACK UP THE HILL, VALERIE GLARES AT – LISA. SUSANNA walks beside her, grinning, oblivious.

                    VALERIE
Did you enjoy the fresh air, Lisa?

                    LISA
Yes I did, Val.

                    VALERIE
                (moving ahead)
Well drink it up, 'cause that was the last goddam time you're
leaving the ward.

                    LISA
Was that a dare or a double dare?

Lisa winks at Susanna. Susanna laughs.

                                        CUT TO:

INT. DANCE THERAPY ROOM – DAY

*MUSIC PLAYS. PAPER CHRISTMAS DECORATIONS ON THE
WINDOWS.* A GROUP INCLUDING SUSANNA, LISA, GEORGINA AND
OTHERS stand in rows. Some look at the ceiling. Some stare in space
– but all lift their arms as instructed by THE DANCE THERAPIST.

                DANCE THERAPIST
Lifting branches up to the sky. That's it. Your leaves dancing
in the breeze.

She continues.

SUSANNA looks to LISA, who wears a sour expression, arms slung
in the air. She makes claws – miming Julie Newmar.

                    LISA
Me-ow.

They laugh. Suddenly Susanna notices:

THROUGH THE WINDOW – OUT IN THE SNOW – DAISY AND HER
DAD, LOADING INTO THEIR CAR. VALERIE HUGS DAISY GOODBYE.

SUSANNA DROPS HER ARMS, WATCHING. One by one – POLLY,
GEORGINA, CYNTHIA, JANET – EACH GIRL DROPS HER ARMS,
WATCHING, SADLY, OUT THE WINDOW. LISA SNEERS:

Good luck, crazy bitch.

JANET SITS DOWN ON THE MAT AND BEGINS TO CRY.

> JANET
> It's not fair. Seventy-four is the perfect weight. *It's not fair!*

> DANCE THERAPIST
> Now. What kind of tree can you be, Janet, down there on the floor?

> JANET
> *I'm a fucking shrub, alright!?*

CLOSE ON: SUSANNA'S EYES – AS DAISY'S CAR DRIVES OFF.

> CUT TO:

INT. SOUTH BELL – LISA'S ROOM – LATE AFTERNOON

BARBIES hang from the ceiling by their necks. The room is a mess of graffiti, clothes, and mutilated stuffed animals. SUSANNA sits on the bed, reading a magazine as –

LISA moves about the room, digging through crap, smoking. *Click, swish.* LILLIAN opens the door.

> LILLIAN
> Checks.

Swish, click – she is gone.

Lisa pulls out SUSANNA'S RED JOURNAL from a magazine pile. She reads aloud from it as Susanna looks up, stricken:

> LISA
> 'Lisa is funny – and terrifying. The staff fears her. She has beautiful red nails. Valerie cut them, said they were "sharps". *That means dangerous.*' I love my section.

> SUSANNA
> *Where did you get that?*
> (stern)
> *Give it to me!*

78

LISA

Hold on. This part's good.
(flipping pages, reading)
'Polly's never unhappy in her tight burnt slipcover skin. Kind
– comforting – cheerful – she's faultless, *like an angel.*
Whatever shadow drove her, whispered "DIE" in her once
perfect ear. Unlike the rest of us – Polly burnt it away. *Fried it.*
(looking up)
That shit's good. Pictures are cool, too.

Lisa holds up A PENCIL DRAWING OF POLLY AND JANET.

SUSANNA

Can I have it back, please?

Lisa hands her the journal. Susanna moves to leave but Lisa
blocks her, rolling up her sleeve, cig hanging on her lip.

LISA

Check this out. That's Ruby. *Meow.*

Lisa proudly displays a cigarette-scarred forearm to Susanna. The
scars form A POINTILLIST PICTURE OF A CAT – IN PROGRESS.

SUSANNA

'Doesn't it hurt?

LISA TOUCHES THE BURNING END OF HER CIGARETTE TO HER
ARM. *It hisses as* IT BURNS IN A FURTHER PIECE OF THE CAT'S
TAIL.

LISA

It passes time.

CUT TO:

WE ARE: INT. MELVIN'S OFFICE – DAY

MELVIN at his desk, explaining:

MELVIN

Scientifically speaking, a *mood* comes from a compound – a
compound of neurotransmitters.

SUSANNA, draped on the couch, plays with a CLOWN PUPPET.

SUSANNA

– *chemicals* –

Melvin nods. *Susanna smiles at Melvin, almost flirtatiously:*

Too much of one, not enough of another, you might set
yourself on fire – or eat too much chicken.

MELVIN

It's not that simple.

SUSANNA

What about a memory?
                    (making the puppet talk)
What's that, Mr Whoopee?

MELVIN

You know what a memory is, Susanna.

SUSANNA

That's not what I mean, Melvin. I mean – what *exactly* is a
memory – in your mind – what is it? *A bunch of cells?*

MELVIN

We *think* it's a pattern of *cellular changes*. In certain areas of
your brain. *We're still learning.*

SUSANNA

You're still learning.

MELVIN

Yes.

SUSANNA

But you're treating us anyway. Giving us drugs and shit – like
you know what you're *doing*.

MELVIN

We know what works, Susanna. Some things we know for
sure.

SUSANNA

How?

MELVIN

From *experience.*

SUSANNA

How do you know Daisy got better?

MELVIN

I don't want to talk about other patients. I want to talk about
you.

SUSANNA

I want to talk about *Daisy.*
How do you know she got better?

MELVIN

No one gets *better*, Susanna – you just make *progress.* Daisy's
progress came from talking – *as will yours* – not about science
or other people, but talking about *yourself* and *your feelings.*

SUSANNA

And from this *talking*, you figure out the thing in my past that
made me this way. Right? *You find my secret.* And how ever
long it takes you, I'm stuck here. That's the game, isn't it?

Susanna glares, waiting for an answer.

Melvin looks at her, very calm.

MELVIN

Do you have your diaphragm in?

SUSANNA

What?!

Two alternating organ notes rise.

IT IS NOT MELVIN AT THE DESK ANYMORE, BUT –

A FLIRTATIOUS BRITISH TEACHER. WE ARE: INT. FACULTY
OFFICE

BRITISH TEACHER

I understand, Susanna, that you come to your student teacher
meetings – *prepared.*

81

Strings rise – minor-keyed. SUSANNA CLOSES HER EYES. *Drums churn out a beat. We hear The Beatles' 'I Am the Walrus'.*

MUSIC CONTINUES. TREES BUDDING – FLOWERS BLOOM – RAIN

PULLING BACK FROM THE TV ROOM WINDOWS –

MARGIE PASSES THROUGH FRAME, CARRYING A MEDICATION TRAY.

WE FOLLOW HER ON HER ROUNDS AS SHE HANDS OUT PILL CUPS.

'I Am the Walrus' plays in the background.

LISA, POLLY, JANET, DUTIFULLY SWALLOWING THEIR PILLS.

ON THE TV: AN UPDATE ON THE WAR. *Dan Rather in a rice paddy.*

CLOSE ON: SUSANNA'S JOURNAL – *SCRAWLED WORDS ON THE PAGE.*

THE WORLD DIDN'T STOP SPINNING JUST BECAUSE WE WEREN'T IN IT. As Susanna's pencil madly sketches THE CAT ON LISA'S ARM.

MARGIE ENTERS SUSANNA'S ROOM WITH THE MEDS TRAY.

SUSANNA sits up in bed, and dutifully swallows. Lies back, *feeling the pill's effect*, as 'I Am the Walrus' continues.

MONTAGE: THE WORLD SPINS AT CLAYMOORE – MUSIC CONTINUES

– WATCHING TV – TEARFUL, AS ROBERT KENNEDY IS MURDERED.
– SUSANNA AND MELVIN – BOTH SLEEPING THROUGH THERAPY.
– SUSANNA FLIRTING WITH JOHN – LISA WATCHING, GLEEFUL.
– BUMPER CARS IN THE LOBBY WITH SWIVEL CHAIRS.
– PINNING A PICTURE OF RICHARD NIXON TO MCWILLEY'S ASS.
– SUSANNA PLAYING NORMAL FOR MOM AND DAD – INTRODUCING LISA.
– POLLY POSES AS SUSANNA DRAWS HER PICTURE.

All the preceding images intercut and build with – SUSANNA'S PENCIL, FEVERISHLY SCRAWLING, WORDS, PICTURES.

As the music winds down:

VALERIE ENTERS THE LOBBY WITH A YOUNG MAN, WHO IS
SMILING.

> VALERIE
> Susanna. You have a visitor.

SUSANNA TURNS — JOURNAL ON HER LAP —

She stares — horrified — then, smiles — *flattered.*

IT IS TOBIAS JACOBS. All the other girls turn, wide-eyed — *A CUTE
GUY!* Lisa raises an eyebrow. John watches — jealous.

> SUSANNA
> Hey. How did — *What are you doing here?*

> TOBIAS
> Hey. I'm — I report next week — *I wanted to see you.*

> CUT TO:

INT. SOUTH BELL — SUSANNA AND GEORGINA'S ROOM — DAY

TOBIAS AND SUSANNA are making out on the floor — furiously.
Click, swish. MARGIE opens the door.

> MARGIE
> Checks — *sorry.*

Margie closes the door.

Toby pulls away from Susanna, red-faced.

He stands — but SUSANNA STARTS UNDOING HIS BELT BUCKLE.

> SUSANNA
> No, no. We have ten minutes.

> CUT TO:

INT. SOUTH BELL — HALLWAY — TEN MINUTES LATER

JANET, M-G, AND CYNTHIA are giggling. POLLY has her ear to
Susanna's door. LISA sits in her swivel chair, smoking.

LISA

Torch. *What are you doing?*

Polly rocks on her heels. Impish.

POLLY

– nothing –

LISA

Then why don't you go to your room and do nothing.

Polly suddenly bursts out crying and runs down the hall past –
MARGIE, who approaches with her chipboard, doing checks. Lisa
slides on her chair between Margie *AND SUSANNA'S DOOR.*

Hey, Margie.

MARGIE

Hey, Lisa.

LISA

How's Joe?

MARGIE
(moving around Lisa)

He's fine.

Lisa adjusts her chair, again *blocking Margie.*

Lisa, *I have to do my checks.*

LISA

And to wait five more minutes would be what – *a dereliction of
duty?*

AT THE STATION, VALERIE notices –

Lisa standing up, blocking Margie.

What if I had a punctured artery?

MARGIE

Lisa. Stop it.

LISA

– *What would you do?* Ignore my wound? Go on about your
appointed rounds?

84

Margie tries to move past Lisa – but Lisa takes the pen from Margie's clipboard and holds it to her neck.

>   If you move one more inch –
>   *I will jam this into my fucking aorta.*

Valerie grabs the pen – from behind.

                    VALERIE
        Your aorta's in your chest.

Valerie crosses to Susanna's door – opens it.
TANGLED AND HALF-DRESSED – SUSANNA AND TOBY FALL OVER.

>   You have grounds privileges, Susanna. Why don't you two
>   take a walk?

                                        CUT TO:

INT. SOUTH BELL – REAR IRON STAIRS – LATE AFTERNOON

SUSANNA AND TOBY CLOMP DOWN THE REAR STAIRS.
Pulling on her coat, Susanna runs her fingers over the iron bars of the railing. WE PAN WITH HER HAND – letting go as HER HAND RUNS OVER – A SHARP PIECE OF METAL.

                                        CUT TO:

EXT. SOUTH BELL – LATE AFTERNOON

SUSANNA bundles up. TOBY pulls up his collar. He takes Susanna's hand and veers their steps toward the parking lot.

                    SUSANNA
        The cafeteria's that way.

                    TOBIAS
        – *keep walking* – Those are my wheels up ahead.

They approach HIS RED BEETLE.

Susanna looks back to – THE WARD. She lets go of Toby's hand.

                    SUSANNA
        What are you doing?

They're at the car. Tobias opens the door for her. Smiles.

> TOBIAS

We're going to Canada.

She looks at the car, at him – smiling sadly – and at the road leading down the hill toward town.

> Susanna. *You're not crazy.*
> You don't need to be here.

> SUSANNA

I tried to kill myself.

> TOBIAS

You took some aspirin.

> SUSANNA

A bottle.

> TOBIAS

And that buys you a year in this joint? Bullshit. They're breaking you. It's nineteen sixty-eight. Everything's *changing*! *What do they know about normal?*

Susanna looks back at South Bell.

LISA AND POLLY STAND IN THE WINDOW. WATCHING.

> SUSANNA

I have friends here, Toby.

> TOBIAS

Who – them? *Those girls?*

Susanna stares at the wet ground beneath her feet.

BLOOD DRIPS INTO A PUDDLE – diffusing into a slick swirl.

HER HAND IS CUT ON THE PALM – BLEEDING. It is a small wound – but Susanna stares at it.

> Susanna – they're eating grapes off the wallpaper. They're *insane*!

> SUSANNA

– if they are – *I am* –

TOBIAS

Come with me. *Please, Susanna.*
– *I think I love you.*

Susanna looks at him – stunned. She laughs – then – suddenly
begins to weep. Toby reached for HER HAND – *BUT SHE PULLS
AWAY FIERCELY. She shields her face, crying.*

My dad gave me five grand. *We can build a cabin in the woods.
We can be happy up there.*

Susanna laughs – long past this kind of fantasy.

You want to leave – *don't you?*

SUSANNA

I do.

(looking up)

– *but not with you.*

This hits Toby hard. He looks away. Susanna smiles gently as hot
tears run down her cheeks. Their eyes meet.

CUT TO:

INT./EXT. SOUTH BELL – AT THE WINDOWS

LISA through the glass. Riveted, watching –

SUSANNA AND TOBY in the parking lot.

POLLY WATCHES TOO – WET-EYED, AT HER WINDOW – AS:

TOBY'S CAR DISAPPEARS. SUSANNA TRUDGES BACK TO THE
WARD.

POLLY'S EYES MOVE TO HER OWN REFLECTION ON THE GLASS.
She stares at herself – *touching her curdled skin.*

POLLY

– my face, *my face* –

CUT TO:

INT. SUSANNA AND GEORGINA'S ROOM – NIGHT

GEORGINA sleeps, soundly.

JOHN quietly fixes a ceiling light from a ladder.

SUSANNA lies on her side, noiselessly SPITTING OUT PILLS,
dropping them in the heater vent.

When John glances at her – *she pretends she's asleep.*
He goes back to work, fastening a metal cage over the bulb.
Susanna opens her eyes again.

John's pants are falling down. He pulls at them. *She smiles.*

He quietly climbs off the ladder and looks at Susanna.
She is 'asleep'. He steps toward her bed, standing over her.
A breeze blows in the window. Crickets sing.

HE GENTLY TUCKS HER IN, then takes the ladder – snaps off the
light – and moves quietly away.

> SUSANNA
> (off-screen)

Why did you do that?

John stops in his tracks – turns.

> *– fix a light bulb at night?*

> JOHN

I'm not here in the morning. And that's when you draw
pictures and stuff.

> SUSANNA

–oh–

John opens the door, heading out.

> . . . *John?*

He stops again, his back to her.

> *– Why do you like me? –*

John turns. *SUSANNA'S EYES ARE FILLED WITH TEARS.*

JOHN

I just like you – *that's all.*
I wish you were getting better. I'd take you to the movies
or something. *Someday.*

There is a silence. *Susanna smiles too.*

SUSANNA

– that'd be nice.

She wipes her tears away.

Suddenly there is a shriek from down the hall.

POLLY
(off-screen)
My face! My face! My faaaaace!

JOHN HEADS OFF TOWARD THE SOUND. MCWILLEY RUSHES PAST.
*The screams continue – and Susanna listens wide-eyed to the off-screen
radio play: a loud clatter as Polly's restrained. Doors are slammed and
her misery suddenly muffled.*

RADIO
*And the smoke of their torment ascendeth up forever and ever –
and the smoke of their . . .*

Susanna looks to Georgina – fast asleep. She rolls into her pillow.
Covering her head.

CUT TO:

INT. SOUTH BELL – HALLWAY – LATER

Down the hall – Polly wails inconsolably, muffled.

SUSANNA steps out of her room, sleepy-eyed.

LISA sits in a swivel chair – 'awake', at least her eyes are open –
spinning the chair in soporific circles.

SUSANNA
What happened?

LISA
What needs to happen? No one's ever gonna kiss her, man.

89

Lisa looks toward the television.

ON THE SCREEN – A MAP OF FLORIDA. IMAGES OF WALT DISNEY, MAPS AND CONSTRUCTION EQUIPMENT.

> 'building a new Disneyland – in Florida. If I could have any job in the world – I'd be a professional Cinderella. *You could be Snow White.*

Susanna snorts a laugh. Lisa looks toward the seclusion room. *Polly's muffled sobbing continues.*

> Polly could be Minnie Mouse. Everyone would be hugging her. No one would even know – 'cause she'd be inside that head.

SUSANNA smiles sadly – looks toward:

MCWILLEY SLUMPED OVER – ASLEEP – IN THE NURSES' STATION.

LISA'S EYES MEET SUSANNA'S.

>   SUSANNA
> Gimme your keys.

Susanna takes the keys and crosses down the hall. Lisa watches Susanna – then crosses to THE NURSES' STATION.

MCWILLEY IS SNORING – BREATHING THROUGH AN OPEN MOUTH.

>   CUT TO:

INT. ART ROOM

SUSANNA LOADS HER ARMS WITH MUSICAL INSTRUMENTS.

>   CUT TO:

INT. NURSES' STATION

LISA CRUMBLES SEVERAL PILLS INTO HER PALM.

SHE LEANS IN THE DUTCH DOOR OF THE NURSES' STATION AND *– DROPS THE POWDER INTO MCWILLEY'S MOUTH.*

>   CUT TO:

INT. SOUTH BELL – OUTSIDE SECLUSION ROOM – NIGHT

Polly's still CRYING. INSTRUMENTS FALL TO THE FLOOR. LISA
smirks as SUSANNA, awkwardly straps on A GUITAR.

SHE PEERS IN THE LITTLE SECLUSION WINDOW.

> SUSANNA
> I don't see her.
> (whispering)
> Hey – Polly. It's Susanna.

Polly continues crying.

> LISA
> Just play something. If talking did shit, we'd all be out of here
> by now.

Susanna sits down on the floor and strums, finding chords. She
sings 'Downtown' in an imperfect but pretty voice.

Susanna glares – Lisa joins in.

Polly becomes quiet.

GEORGINA CROSSES TO HER DOOR, PEERING DOWN THE
HALLWAY. DOWN THE HALL – LISA AND SUSANNA PASSIONATELY
SERENADE POLLY. GEORGINA JOINS IN.

JANET AND CYNTHIA LIE AWAKE IN BED. LISTENING. THEY JOIN
IN.

JOHN'S FEET WALK BRISKLY TOWARD – SUSANNA AND LISA.

John stands above the girls, arms folded.

> JOHN
> McWilley's gonna wake up.

The girls continue singing.

John looks cute when he's pissed.

Susanna beckons him with her finger. He leans down and –
SUSANNA TAKES HIS FACE IN HER HANDS AND KISSES HIM.

Lisa takes the guitar and continues singing as:

M-G BOUNDS DOWN THE HALL, JOINING LISA AS:

JOHN AND SUSANNA MAKE OUT ON THE FLOOR.

                                                    CUT TO:

INT. SOUTH BELL – SECLUSION ROOM – LATER

Pink sunrise seeps in the transom window. POLLY is huddled in a corner – in a strait-jacket – quietly singing 'Downtown'.

                                                    CUT TO:

INT. SOUTH BELL – DAWN

Pale pink dawn light. SUSANNA IS CURLED UP IN JOHN'S ARMS. She wakes, spying Valerie stomping off her feet in the lobby.

LISA is out cold on the floor. M-G, spooning with her.

Susanna pries herself away from John – he wakes, and their eyes meet. She smiles tenderly – and scurries away.

VALERIE STANDS OVER MCWILLEY ASLEEP ON THE FLOOR OF THE NURSES' STATION. She looks down the hall just as – *Susanna disappears into her room.*

                                                    CUT TO:

INT. SOUTH BELL – SUSANNA AND GEORGINA'S ROOM

SUSANNA in her bed – feigns sleep.

VALERIE – arms folded – in the doorway, pissed off.

                          VALERIE
          I have to write this up, Susanna. I am *tired* of this bullshit.

                                                    CUT TO:

INT. DOCTOR WICK'S OUTER OFFICE – DAY

SUSANNA sits in a vinyl chair, exhausted. Beside her, MARGIE.

ARLEEN reads THE MARILYN MONROE *LIFE* MAGAZINE (that the Security Guard was reading at Wick's desk).

                    DR WICK
                  (off-screen)
   Is she here?

                                              CUT TO:

INT. DR WICK'S OFFICE – DAY

SUSANNA pushes open the door. It is dark inside. The only light
seeping through the blinds. Clouds of cigarette smoke.

Susanna sees – THE CRACKED WALLPAPER IN THE CORNER. *The
shape of Florida.*

A WOMAN (sixty) WITH BRIGHT-GREEN EYES SITS IN THE
SHADOWS. Behind a desk. Smoking. Reading Susanna's file. There
is a precision to her manner. Susanna sits in a leather chair.

The deskplate reads – *S. G. WICK, MD.* The woman speaks
without looking up. Her accent – *South African.*

                    DR WICK
   Good morning, Susanna.

                    SUSANNA
   Good morning.

                    DR WICK
   How are you?

                    SUSANNA
   Fine – I guess.

Dr Wick looks up from the file.

                    DR WICK
   You look tired.

                    SUSANNA
   I am.

                    DR WICK
   Why is that?

                    SUSANNA
   Polly went crazy last night and we sang to her – Lisa and me.

                       93

DR WICK

Did it soothe her? Your singing.

SUSANNA

She stopped crying.

DR WICK

Have you become friends with Lisa?

SUSANNA

Why – is that bad?

DR WICK

Does it feel bad?

SUSANNA

No.

DR WICK

Did you have many girlfriends – before you came here?

SUSANNA

Not really.

DR WICK

Would you say before you came here your friends consisted mainly of boyfriends? Men?

Susanna lights a cig – looks at the folder in Wick's hand.

SUSANNA

Does it say in there I'm promiscuous?

DR WICK

Why did you choose that word?

SUSANNA

Should I say *horny*?

DR WICK

You should say what you mean. Do you consider yourself promiscuous?

SUSANNA

No – but you do.

DR WICK

What makes you think that?

SUSANNA

How many guys would I have to sleep with to be
promiscuous? Text-book promiscuous.

DR WICK

What do you think?

SUSANNA

Ten? Eight? Five?

Wick does not react.

How many girls would a boy my age have to sleep with to be
promiscuous? Ten? Twenty? A hundred and nine?

DR WICK

Someone who is compulsively promiscuous might engage in a
sex act with a guest in their room and then engage in another
sex act on the same day with an orderly.

Susanna is stunned. Then laughs.

SUSANNA

John? All I did was kiss him. Am I in trouble for kissing an
orderly or giving my boyfriend a blow job?

DR WICK

Is there something about sex that grounds you? Lifts your
feelings of despair?

SUSANNA

Yes.

DR WICK

What is that?

SUSANNA

Have you ever had sex?

Wick says nothing. *The clock ticks loudly.*

This is called 'resistance', isn't it, – what I'm giving you?

DR WICK

Resistance is revealing. Freud thought analysis was essentially the analysis of a patient's resistance to analysis.

SUSANNA

Oh, did he?

DR WICK

Melvin says you have many interesting theories about your illness. You believe there's a mystical undertow in life –
(reading)
– 'a quicksand of shadows'.

SUSANNA

Another one of my theories is that you guys don't know what you're doing.

DR WICK

Still – you acknowledge a problem. Coping with this *quicksand*.

SUSANNA

I have a problem coping with this hospital. I want to leave.

DR WICK

I can't do that.

SUSANNA

I signed myself in. I want to sign myself out.

DR WICK

You signed yourself *into our care*. *We* decide when to release you. You're not ready, Susanna.

SUSANNA

Because I won't finger paint or pretend I'm a tree?

DR WICK

Your progress has plateaued.

Susanna receives this, unblinking.

That disappoints you?

SUSANNA

Not really. I'm ambivalent. That's my new favorite word, in
fact. Ambivalent.

DR WICK

Do you know what it means? Ambivalence. Text-book
ambivalence.

SUSANNA

I don't care.

DR WICK

If it's your favorite word, I would think that you –

SUSANNA

It means – I don't care. *That's what it means.*

DR WICK

On the contrary, Susanna. Ambivalence suggests strong
feelings. In opposition. The prefix – like in ambi-dextrous –
(raising her hands)
– means 'both'. The rest, from Latin, means vigor. The word
suggests you're torn between two opposing courses of action.

SUSANNA

Will I stay – or will I go?

DR WICK

Am I sane or – or am I crazy?

SUSANNA

Those aren't courses of action.

DR WICK

They can be, dear – *for some.*

SUSANNA

Well, I guess it's the wrong word then.

DR WICK

No – I think it's perfect.

The clock seems to tick even louder.

It's a very big question you're faced with, Susanna. The

choice of your life. How much will you indulge your flaws? Are your flaws, your music, your identity? If you embrace them – as one should embrace their identity – then you may commit yourself to life in hospital. Big questions. Big choices. Only natural you'd profess carelessness about them.

Susanna stands. Stubs out her cigarette.

> SUSANNA
>
> . . . Is that it?

> DR WICK
>
> For now.

Susanna slams the door.

CUT TO:

INT. ADMINISTRATION BUILDING – STAIRS – DAY

MARGIE walks with SUSANNA. Susanna is very *pissed.*

COMING UP THE HALL – GRETTA ESCORTS LISA. *As they pass – Susanna looks into Lisa's eyes.*

Lisa looks, sluggish, drugged.

GRETTA TAKES LISA ROUND THE CORNER – INTO WICK'S OFFICE.

CUT TO:

INT. SOUTH BELL – TV ROOM – DAY

SUSANNA sits, staring – dead-eyed – at the TV.

> GEORGINA
>
> She's been a zombie for three days.

POLLY – looking much better – stands with GEORGINA.

They stare at Susanna. Polly approaches her.

> POLLY
>
> Hey. Susanna.

Susanna does not react. *Valerie crosses past, watching.*

Daisy sent us a postcard of her apartment. She got a pussy cat.

Susanna turns. Glassy-eyed. Distant.

                    SUSANNA
– *Where's Lisa?*

                    POLLY
They – they put her in another ward. She'll be back though. She always is.

Susanna rocks her head back on the couch. Polly backs away.
LOOKING BACKWARD TOWARD THE TV ROOM WINDOWS, SUSANNA SEES:

RUSHING GREEN LEAVES OUT A CAR WINDOW (FLASHBACK).

REVERSE ON: BABY SUSANNA, strapped to a board in the back of a station wagon, staring upward at the rushing world.

                                        CUT TO:

INT. SOUTH BELL – SUSANNA'S ROOM – LATER

LIGHT FILTERS THROUGH SUSANNA'S WINDOW.

SUSANNA in a smock, in a fetal position, stares out of her window. Her hair stringy. She examines her limp hand.

                    VALERIE
I think you need to get up.

                    SUSANNA
I'm just going to rest for a while.

VALERIE PICKS SUSANNA UP LIKE A RAG DOLL.

What the hell are you doing? Put me down! Put me DOWN!

                                        CUT TO:

INT. HALLWAY/STAIRS

VALERIE purposefully carries SUSANNA down the hall as Susanna SCREAMS AND YELLS. NURSES dodge out of the way as Valerie hauls Susanna down the stairs.

INT. THE HYDROTHERAPY ROOM

VALERIE DUMPS SUSANNA IN A BIG BATH TUB. SPLASH!

> SUSANNA
>
> *AAAHHH SHIT!*

> VALERIE
>
> I'm sorry, *is it too cold?*

> SUSANNA
>
> *GET ME OUT OF THIS FUCKING TUB!*

Susanna stands up in the tub, drenched, crying out.

> *GET ME OUT OF THIS TUB, YOU BITCH!*

> VALERIE
>
> *GET YOURSELF OUT OF THE TUB!*

> SUSANNA
>
> WHERE THE FUCK IS *LISA!? WHERE'S LISA!?*

> VALERIE
>
> I have no idea. *'Think you can survive without her?*

> SUSANNA
>
> *YOU BANISH HER FOR SINGING TO POLLY?! WE WERE TRYING TO HELP HER! THIS PLACE IS A FASCIST TORTURE CHAMBER!*

> VALERIE
>
> NO BABY, THIS IS A *4 STAR HOTEL!*

Susanna starts singing *Porgy and Bess.*

> I can take a lot of *SHIT* from crazy people – but *YOU ARE NOT CRAZY!*

> SUSANNA
>
> *THEN WHAT THE FUCK IS WRONG WITH ME?! WHAT THE FUCK IS GOING ON IN MY HEAD?*

Valerie does not reply.

Tell me, Doctor Val! Give me your diag-nonsense!

VALERIE

In my opinion. You are a *fool* – indulging her little self.

SUSANNA

Oh. Is that your *MEDICAL OPINION?!* Based upon your
advanced studies at a night school for welfare mothers!?

VALERIE

*YOU IGNORANT GIRL! WAKE THE FUCK UP!! YOU ARE
GIVING IT AWAY!*

SUSANNA	VALERIE
Melvin doesn't have a clue!	*YOU ARE THROWING IT*
Wick is a psycho! and *YOU* –	*AWAY, GIRL!*

SUSANNA

– YOU PRETEND YOU'RE A DOCTOR – YOU READ CHARTS AND
DOLE OUT MEDS – BUT YOUZ AIN'T NO DOCTOR, MISS
VALERIE. *YOUZ AIN'T NOTHIN' BUT A BLACK NURSE MAID!*

A beat. Eyes locked. Then, Valerie walks out. *The door slams.*

GET ME OUT OF HERE!

Susanna stands there, dripping cold. She climbs out of the tub,
clinging to the rails. She walks across the tile, shivering, and grabs
A ROBE.

CUT TO:

INT. SOUTH BELL – SUSANNA'S ROOM – NIGHT

Crickets sing. Moonlight. SUSANNA sleeps in her bed.

A creak. SHE OPENS HER EYES.

LISA STANDS OVER HER, SHROUDED IN DARKNESS. SHE SMILES –
but there is a desperation in her eyes.

LISA

Are you my friend?

Susanna nods. GEORGINA WATCHES IN THE DARKNESS.

    Let's go to Florida.

CUT TO:

LISA LEADS SUSANNA DOWN THE DARK HALL – NIGHT

SUSANNA

We need money, don't we?

LISA

You've been tonguing your pills, right?

Lisa unlocks the art room door.

SUSANNA

But –

LISA SPINS AROUND – THE FIRST TIME WE'VE SEEN HER IN LIGHT.
DESPERATE, WILD-EYED, SHE PINS SUSANNA AGAINST THE WALL.

LISA

I gotta get out of here! They gave me shocks again, Maddy!

SUSANNA

– Susanna. I'm *Susanna*.

CUT TO:

EXT. CLAYMOORE GROUNDS – NIGHT

A CAR approaches, causing LISA AND SUSANNA to hit the ground.
It passes and they scramble to the bottom of the hill, over a fence,
to the TWO-LANE ROAD. Lisa immediately affects a new posture –
carefree. She begins walking backwards, thumb out.

SUSANNA

What are we doing?

Lisa hands Susanna a wadded envelope. Susanna opens it.

    'Please give Daisy Randazzo assistance installing a telephone
at 23 Revere, #4. It's important for us to have access to one
another via telephone.'

A CAR APPROACHES. *vvvRRRMMMmmmmm.* And passes.

I thought we were going to Florida.

> LISA
> It's a place to crash – till we get plane tickets.

Lisa grins as A VW VAN APPROACHES – *Gram Parsons* blaring –
headlights in her eyes.

THE VAN SLOWS. A sliding door opens – A FRIENDLY OLDER
GROUP. Grinning. TWO GUYS AND A GIRL.

> CUT TO:

INT. VW VAN – TRAVELING – NIGHT

Gram Parsons plays on the eight track.
LISA is in heaven, giddy. She does her nails. Red. She passes the
polish to SUSANNA, who bobs her head to the music.

THE TWO GUYS SIT UP FRONT passing a joint between them. Lisa
takes a toke, offering it to Susanna – who takes some. The DRIVER
nudges the STONED GUY, smoking a joint beside him.

> DRIVER
> Enough time for you?

The Stoned Guy nods, drops two dollars in the Driver's hand.

> He bet me you were escapees from Claymoore. I said, '*No
> fuckin' way.*'

Lisa takes the money out of the Driver's hand.

> LISA
> Womp. You lose.

It's very quiet in the car. Suddenly, LISA, SUSANNA AND THE
OTHERS break into a weed-enhanced laughing jag.

CLOSE ON: SUSANNA looks at Lisa, adoringly.

LISA MEETS SUSANNA'S EYES. They smile at one another, giddy
with adventure. Suddenly, SUSANNA KISSES LISA, on the lips. Lisa
grins, startled – and pleased. They laugh.

> CUT TO:

EXT. BOSTON COFFEE HOUSE – MORNING

SUSANNA and LISA sip coffees. Lisa is beaming with freedom.

> LISA
> Gimme your pills.

Susanna hands over a stash of meds. Lisa sorts them.

> We'll keep a few.
> (beat)
> There's a guy who buys Valium – he hangs out a couple
> blocks from here – by the museum.

Susanna looks up. Lisa lights a cigarette.

> SUSANNA
> What museum?

                                                    CUT TO:

EXT. LARDNER MUSEUM/BY THE RIVER – DAY

Climbing up a hill, coming from A SMALL HIPPY-STYLE
SHANTYTOWN NESTLED BENEATH A BRIDGE, Lisa sucks on a butt,
frustrated. She looks about for her connections.

> LISA
> Shit. It's too early. I don't know where they are.

Susanna leans on a tree, staring at THE LARDNER MUSEUM, across
the street. She watches MUSEUM-GOERS shuffling in.

                                                    CUT TO:

INT. LARDNER MUSEUM – GALLERIES – DAY

LISA sits on a bench, bored to tears. A MUSEUM GUARD watches
her carefully.

SUSANNA wanders through the galleries.

MANY PEOPLE ARE ENGROSSED IN THE ART – BUT SOME SEEM TO
BE LOOKING AT SUSANNA. OLD LADIES, CHILDREN. GUARDS. AND
A YOUNG WOMAN IN A PAINTING.

THE PAINTING – A YOUNG GIRL HAVING A MUSIC LESSON. But she's facing out of the picture – looking at Susanna. Her mouth open as if she were about to say something.

Susanna moves on – and stares admiringly at:

A GIANT FRAMED CANVAS. In the painting, many peasants are staring upward to a hot air balloon, high in the sky.

Susanna smiles to herself. She backs up from it as:

AN ART TEACHER leads TEN WELL-DRESSED PRIVATE SCHOOL SENIORS to a portrait of Hercules holding a big stick.

> ART TEACHER
> (off-screen)
> I believe you all remember Hercules . . .

The teacher continues with the lesson.

Some girls giggle at the painting. Among them, MAUREEN.

Maureen.

> MAUREEN

– sorry –

Two boys notice SUSANNA, who turns away, nonchalant.

> ART TEACHER
> This way. Remember last week when we talked about Vermeer? They've got a good one: *Girl Interrupted at Her Music.*

They congregate around THE PAINTING OF THE STARING GIRL.

What do you think, Jack?

> BOY I (JACK)

I wouldn't kick her out of bed.

A bunch of boys laugh. CONNIE, obnoxious, raises her hand.

> ART TEACHER
> What do you think, Connie?
> First impressions.

                              CONNIE
I saw it already – in a book.

                           ART TEACHER
But what do you think of it *in person*?

                              CONNIE
It's small.

                           ART TEACHER
Tiffany?

                             TIFFANY
It's that muted Flemish kind of light.

                           ART TEACHER
Forget the encyclopedia. What do you think she's saying? The
girl.

Susanna infiltrates the group, curious.

                             TIFFANY
Get me some new hair?

                           ART TEACHER
What do you think, Maureen?

Maureen stands directly beside Susanna. She looks back at the
painting. Thoughtful.

                             MAUREEN
– I think her teacher's pissed –
                         (some kids laugh)
He's trying to get her attention, but she's looking out. As if –
I don't know –

                           ART TEACHER
What?

Maureen turns, meeting eyes with Susanna.

                             MAUREEN
. . . as if she's trying to get out of the painting.

CLOSE ON: SUSANNA – disturbed, looking up at:

                              106

THE PAINTING. THE STARING GIRL. THE PIANO.

The sound of a piano rises.

SUSANNA TURNS – SHE IS IN A DARK HOUSE.

An off-screen piano – *A CHOPIN POLONAISE.*

WE ARE: INT. KAYSEN HOUSE – HALLWAY – NIGHT (FLASHBACK)

THE DOG sleeps beneath an armchair. *The music continues.*

One awkward passage of music is repeated over and over.

SUSANNA moves past the dog, toward the Library. *A frustrated slam of the piano keys. Then the music resumes.* SUSANNA rounds a corner, ENTERS THE LIBRARY.

HER MOTHER sits in the dark, playing piano. A bourbon by the keyboard. She stops – looks up –

> ANNETTE
> . . . I played that once. In a concert – at the Conservatory. Ages ago.

> SUSANNA
> Why did you stop playing?

> ANNETTE
> Well . . . I had a child, didn't I?

Annette goes back to playing.

> SUSANNA
> Where's Dad?

> ANNETTE
> Thesis review.
> (smiles, sadly)
> We're on our own tonight. You need to go to market. Get us some steaks.

A HAND JERKS SUSANNA'S SHOULDER

WE ARE: BACK AT THE MUSEUM

> LISA
> Come on. I'm over this joint.

Susanna is spun around. Standing in the gallery. Her eyes filled with emotion. Lisa is concerned.

> SUSANNA
> How long have we –?

> LISA
> Don't come unglued on me.

CUT TO:

EXT. PARK OUTSIDE MUSEUM – BY THE RIVER – DAY

WITH A PACK OF HIPPIES AT THE SHANTYTOWN BENEATH THE BRIDGE, LISA talks with a SEEDY-LOOKING GUY. He just keeps shrugging.

SUSANNA watches from up the hill.

TWO OTHERS FROM THE PACK, HANDSOME BOY and his TOUGH FRIEND eye Susanna from a distance. Susanna turns away.

CUT TO:

INT. DRUG PARTY AT A DILAPIDATED BOSTON HOUSE – NIGHT

TRIPPY MUSIC PLAYS – LOUD. It is crowded with people in tie-dye and ripped T-shirts. A big bong and a haze of smoke. Rainbow-colored lights. This is a stark contrast with the preppie party in Susanna's past.

LISA is working on THE TOUGH GUY – flirting, kissing. She moves with him into THE BACK ROOM.

Susanna is on the couch. HANDSOME BOY (TONY) paws her. He is very high. He climbs into her lap. She giggles.

                              TONY
What.

                            SUSANNA
Tony. *You don't want me.*

                              TONY
Yes, I do, *baaby.*

                            SUSANNA
I'm a crazy girl.

                              TONY
You're crazy – so we can't have one night of bliss?

                            SUSANNA
                            (smiles)
No – I'm really crazy.

                              TONY
'You been in a hospital?

She nods.

    'You see purple people?

She shakes her head.

    My friend, he saw purple people. So, the state, they put him
    away. He didn't like that. So, one day, he told 'em he didn't
    see purple people no more.

                            SUSANNA
He got better.

                              TONY
Nah. He still sees 'em.

LISA STEPS OUT OF THE BACK ROOM.

                              LISA
Come on.

SUSANNA SITS UP AS LISA HOLDS THE DOOR, smiling at Tony –

    We gotta split. *Now.*

SUSANNA FOLLOWS LISA OUT THE DOOR AND DOWN THE HALL.

> CUT TO:

INT./EXT. CITY CAB – NIGHT

SUSANNA watches the lights, rubbing her temples.
LISA fumbles through THE TOUGH GUY'S WALLET.

She finds ten dollars – hands it to the driver – and throws the wallet out of the window.

> LISA

Twenty-three Revere Street.

> CUT TO:

EXT. BOSTON STREET CORNER – REVERE STREET – NIGHT

A quiet block – brownstones converted to apartments. LISA LOOKS FOR THE HOUSE. SUSANNA looks about – spots:

A REAL ESTATE SIGN: *IF YOU LIVED HERE, YOU'D BE HOME BY NOW.*

> CUT TO:

INT. 23 REVERE STREET – BROWNSTONE HALLWAY – #4 – NIGHT

Through the door, a TV is playing – we hear the national anthem.
Susanna knocks. No answer. She knocks again.

> DAISY
> (off-screen)

Identify yourself.

> SUSANNA

It's Susanna and –

Lisa stops her – shakes her head.

It's Susanna. Daisy?

> DAISY
> (off-screen)

It's four o'clock in the morning.

SUSANNA

I know – we – I need someplace to crash.

DAISY
(off-screen)

Say the password.

SUSANNA

What password?

DAISY
(off-screen)

Think of one.

Lisa is laughing, trying to keep it hushed. Susanna thinks.

SUSANNA

McWilley.

The door unlocks. *CLICK*. It opens a crack – chain still on.
WE SEE: DAISY'S EYE LOOKING AT SUSANNA.

DAISY

You got Valium?

Susanna nods. Daisy opens the door – THEN SEES:

LISA

Hey, Daisy.

DAISY TRIES TO CLOSE THE DOOR – *but Lisa has wedged herself.*

Daisy. Peace, man. I wanted to come and say how sorry I was for being a bitch. I was a fucking drag. Please forgive me.

Daisy looks at Lisa, wary.

CUT TO:

INT. DAISY'S STUDIO APARTMENT – NIGHT

Orange shag carpeting. Yellow drapes. Impeccably neat. But it is so dark that there is a bluish caramel color to everything – eerily lit by moonlight and a throbbing television displaying a static shot of the American flag, squawking out '*Stars and Stripes Forever*'.

DAISY locks the door behind them. She wears a terry robe and slippers.

> SUSANNA

Cool pad.

> DAISY

Thanks.

LISA AND SUSANNA stand, uneasy, in the dark room.

DAISY shuffles to the stairs. She turns on the lights.

I'll get some blankets.

> SUSANNA

Let me help.

> DAISY
> (spinning around – firm)

No. Stay here.

Lisa raises an eyebrow to Susanna – moves into the room. She fingers some of Daisy's trinkets on an end table: Porcelain figurines of animals, an antique clock.

Susanna watches Lisa – coveting the delicate knick-knacks.

> SUSANNA

Don't take anything.

IN THE DARKNESS A CHICKEN CARCASS sits on the counter. A GRAY CAT licks at it, its eyes glowing in the shadows.

> LISA

Meow.

> SUSANNA

Here, kitty, kitty.

Lisa crosses – reaching for the cat. IT SPITS. LISA RECOILS. Daisy clomps down the stairs, arms filled with blankets.

> DAISY

That's Ruby. My Dad bought her for me.

                    LISA
You named your cat after my arm.

Daisy drops the blankets on the couch and turns –

                    DAISY
This is a Castro Convertible. It pulls out. The bathroom's there.

Lisa looks in the bathroom.

A MOP PROPPED IN A SMALL SHOWER STALL – AND A TOILET.

                    LISA
Don't you have a tub?

Susanna unfolds the bed – spreading the sheets.

                    DAISY
No – I don't.

                    LISA
What about upstairs?

                    DAISY
No.

Lisa crosses to the refrigerator.

Did you two escape or what?

                    LISA
All you have in here is mustard.

Susanna pulls off her jeans and climbs under the covers.

                    SUSANNA
We're going to Florida tomorrow.

                    DAISY
And what are you gonna do in Florida?

                    LISA
                (closing the fridge)
I'm gonna be a professional Cinderella at Walt Disney's new
theme park. *Susanna's gonna be Snow White.*

Daisy laughs. Lisa searches the cupboard.

                    113

You can come if you want – you could be that Cocker Spaniel that eats spaghetti.

>   (beat)

I want to make pancakes.

>   DAISY

There's a market on the corner.

>   SUSANNA

I want to sleep.

>   LISA

No. In the *morning*.

>   DAISY

Pans are under the sink. Silver's in the drawer.

Lisa pulls open the drawer. A FULL SET OF SILVERWARE. Daisy watches her, washing a glass – filling it with water.

RUBY THE CAT hops up on the fold-out bed. Parks herself in front of Susanna. The cat stares at her. Susanna smiles and reaches out – very gently – towards Ruby. The cat meets her fingers with the side of its head – *purrs*.

Do you guys have any money?
'You got a safety net down there?

Susanna looks up from the cat.

People you know. Relatives.

>   LISA

– yeah –

Daisy decides to press no further. She peels a five from A WAD OF BILLS in her robe pocket and puts it on the counter.

>   DAISY

– for your pancakes. Don't make a lot of noise in the morning. I sleep late. I'll come down when I'm ready.

Lisa eyes Daisy. Daisy smiles, uneasy. Getting impatient.

Gimme the Valium.

                                    LISA
            We don't need your daddy's money.

                                    DAISY
            Then leave it there. Just give me the fucking Valium.

DAISY HOLDS OUT HER HAND.

LISA SIGHS, HOLDING OUT THE PILLS — BUT SUDDENLY NOTICES
— A RED SCAB PEEKING OUT FROM THE SLEEVE OF DAISY'S ROBE.

DAISY REACHES FOR THE PILLS — BUT LISA GRABS DAISY'S
WRIST. DAISY JERKS BACK. HER ROBE SLEEVE *PULLS WAY UP*
AND WE SEE: ALL ALONG HER ARM — *SLASHES — VICIOUS SLASHES
— SCABBED.*

                                    LISA
        What's this?

                                    DAISY
        Let go!

Susanna sits up in bed.

                                    LISA
        Trying out your new silver?

                                    DAISY
        LET FUCKING GO!

                                    SUSANNA
        Lisa!

                                    LISA
        'less appealing for Daddy, huh?

Daisy jerks her arm away. Swallows the pills. *Growls.*

                                    DAISY
        Look at your own arm, *asshole.*

                                    LISA
        I'm *sick*, Daisy – *we know that.* But here you are, in so-called
        'recovery', playing Betty Crocker, cut-up like a goddam
        Virginia ham.

Lisa, stop it!

LISA

Help me understand. Daise. I thought you didn't do Valium.
Tell me how the safety net is working *for you*. Tell me you
don't drag that blade across your skin and pray for the
courage to *press down*. Tell me Daddy helps you cope with
that. *Illuminate me*.

Daisy smiles, tense – speaks very quietly.

DAISY

My father loves me.

LISA

I'll bet. With every inch of his manhood.

Daisy's eyes are black. She speaks with an eerie calm.

DAISY

I'm going to sleep now. Please be gone in the morning.
            (back to Lisa, proud, plain)
You're just jealous, Lisa – because I was released. 'Cause I
got better. 'Cause I have a chance – *at a life*.

LISA

            (smiles, amused)
They didn't release you because you're *better*, Daisy. They –
just – gave – up.

Daisy moves to the stairs. Her back to Lisa.

You call this a life? This? Taking Daddy's money – buying
doilies and knick-knacks – eating his chicken – fattening up
like a prize heifer. Y'changed the scenery, baby, not the
situation. The Warden makes fucking *housecalls*.
            (deliberate, almost serene)
Everyone – knows – he – fucks – you.

Halfway up the stairs, Daisy stops, head down.

What – they – don't – know –

116

SUSANNA

SHUT THE FUCK UP!

LISA

– is that you *like it*.
(eyes blazing, with a smile)
Hey. That's okay. It's only natural. *A man is a dick is a man is
a dick is a chicken is a dad, a valium, a speculum, a cucumber –
what-ever*. It's all the same. You – like – being – Mrs
Randazzo.
(with disdain)
Probably all you've ever known.

Daisy rubs her head. Turns away. Her body collapsing as she
mounts the last steps.

DAISY

Have fun in Florida.

THE DOOR UPSTAIRS CLOSES. Lisa looks to:

SUSANNA, who crosses to the bathroom and SLAMS THE DOOR.

CUT TO:

INT. DAISY'S DOWNSTAIRS BATHROOM – NIGHT

RED-EYED, HYPER-VENTILATING, SUSANNA opens the medicine
cabinet. Men's stuff: *Vitalis, Noxema shave cream, Brut deodorant.*

We hear a distant piano. Rubbing her temples, Susanna finds:

A BOTTLE OF ASPIRIN. *But it's empty. The door knob jiggles.*

LISA
(off-screen)
Susanna. Come on. Open the door.

Susanna does not reply. She curls up in the shower stall. Water
drips from the shower head onto her shoes. *Drip. Drop.*

YOUNG SUSANNA
(off-screen)
*One, two, buckle my shoe –
three, four, close the door –*

117

Susanna turns, sees:

HERSELF, ON THE FLOOR OF HER BEDROOM, PLAYING JACKS

CLOSER: WE SEE SHE IS PLAYING JACKS WITH ASPIRIN TABLETS.

> YOUNG SUSANNA
> *Five, six, pick up sticks –*

Susanna tosses the ball up, scoops tablets, catches the ball, pops the aspirins into her mouth, washes them down with vodka.

Downstairs, the piano playing stops cold. Another go. This time Susanna misses the ball. *It rolls across the floor –*

STOPPED BY AN EMPTY 50-TABLET ASPIRIN BOTTLE.

SUSANNA'S FACE HITS THE FLOOR. Fading, she stares at:

A SPIDER'S WEB under the dresser. A BEETLE STRUGGLES – tangled.

> ANNETTE
> (off-screen)
> Susanna are you going to the market or not?! I asked you an hour ago!

SUSANNA PUTS HER HAND TO HER MOUTH – queasy.

> CUT TO:

INT. DAISY'S STUDIO APARTMENT – DAWN

The pink light of sunrise seeps through the window.
LISA SLEEPS in a tangle – on the couch.
California Dreamin' plays upstairs. Loud.

SUSANNA emerges from the bathroom. Pale.

She moves quietly past Lisa.

SHE TAKES DAISY'S FIVE-DOLLAR BILL from the counter.

> CUT TO:

EXT. 23 REVERE STREET – MORNING

SUSANNA steps out of the building. *A plane flies overhead.*
RUBY THE CAT tries to follow but she shuts the door – hard.

Susanna steps into the sun. Numb. She walks toward – A BODEGA
MARKET ON THE CORNER.

RUBY runs out from a side alley, and leaps on to the front steps,
watching through the railing as Susanna walks on.

                                                    CUT TO:

INT. CORNER MARKET – MORNING

A small bodega-type shop. SUSANNA stands in an aisle, holding a
basket filled with bacon, eggs and milk, staring at AUNT JEMIMAH
pancake mix. Susanna takes the box and notices:

A HOLE IN THE SHELVES. Through the hole we see PROFESSOR
GILCREST in the next aisle, pushing a cart in A BRIGHTER
SUPERMARKET.

BACK TO: SUSANNA AT THE SHELF wearing the same clothes from
the aspirin/jacks scene. She too now stands, woozy, in THE
BIGGER BRIGHTER SUPERMARKET. She backs away from Gilcrest,
checking the grocery list in her hand.

It reads: *TWO SIRLOINS*

SUSANNA crosses shakily to the MEAT SECTION. She picks up a
wrapped steak but pulls away, horrified, as she feels BLOOD ON
HER FINGERS. She stares down at:

BLOOD FILLS THE CELLOPHANE-WRAPPED MEAT PACKAGE. IT
BURSTS FROM THE WRAPPER AND STARTS GUSHING FROM THE
SURROUNDING PACKAGES. BLOOD FILLS THE DISPLAY, RUNNING
OVER ON TO THE LINOLEUM. A PUDDLE SPREADS AROUND HER
FEET.

Susanna cries, about to collapse, and looks up, toward:

                    PROFESSOR GILCREST
    Susanna?!

PROFESSOR GILCREST at the end of the aisle.
He moves toward Susanna as:

SUSANNA'S LEGS FOLD. SHE SINKS TO THE FLOOR LIKE A RAG
DOLL.

> ITALIAN LADY
> (off-screen)
> Can I help you, dear?

PRESENT SUSANNA TURNS – OVERWHELMED BY HER VISION.
A broken bottle of maple syrup at her feet.

SHE IS BACK IN THE SMALL BODEGA AND A SQUAT SHOP OWNER
(ITALIAN LADY) STANDS BEFORE HER.

> CUT TO:

INT. DAISY'S STUDIO APARTMENT – MORNING

SUSANNA enters – drops the bag on the counter.
LISA makes coffee. Susanna refuses to look at her.
Upstairs, California Dreamin' still plays.

> SUSANNA
> – has she come down?

> LISA
> (shakes her head)
> 'been playing that shit all morning.

RUBY THE CAT sits on the stairs. *Meow.* Susanna turns. The cat
runs up the steps.

> CUT TO:

INT. DAISY'S – UPSTAIRS – OUTSIDE DAISY'S ROOM – MORNING

The Mamas and Papas blast through the door.

> SUSANNA
> Daisy – *Daisy?*

Dread washes over Susanna. She opens the door. The room is

120

empty. Just a turntable on repeat, playing a Mamas and Papas forty-five. *The song starts again.*

Susanna turns. RUBY THE CAT sits at THE BATHROOM DOOR.

Susanna pushes it open. *Drip. Drop.*

Blood drips into TWO DARK POOLS ON THE TILE.

Hanging from the overhead fixture:

DAISY HAS CUT HER WRISTS AND HANGED HERSELF WITH A BELT. SUSANNA GASPS FOR AIR. She holds on to the door to keep from keeling over. Her face ashen, her breathing labored, her gag reflex contracting. *The Mamas and Papas keep playing . . .*

> LISA
>
> What an idiot.

Lisa stands at the door; hardly reacts at all. A bare flicker of emotion in her eyes, she stares at Daisy's lifeless body.

Susanna stumbles to Daisy's room – to the phone . . . dials.

> SUSANNA
> (into phone)
> Hello – I need an ambulance!

> LISA
>
> Make it a hearse.

> SUSANNA
> (into phone)
> I think she killed herself. *Daisy – Daisy Randazzo – Revere Street. The address? Um.* Twenty –

> LISA
>
> – three –

> SUSANNA
> (into phone)
> Twenty-three Revere – Yes! *Please, hurry!*

Susanna hangs up as – LISA steps around the blood. She kicks the cat away and reaches into Daisy's robe. Daisy's body swings gently. Lisa finds THE WAD OF BILLS.

You pressed all her buttons – and now you're taking her money.

Lisa pads out of the bathroom. She looks Susanna in the eye.

LISA

I didn't press shit. She was waiting for an excuse.

Lisa tucks the cash in Susanna's breast pocket – she moves to the stairs.

Pack up. We have to get out of here. Luckily, we have cash.

Susanna turns from Lisa in disgust – she sits down in the bathroom doorway. Tears run down her face.

Susanna. Don't be stupid.

Susanna looks at Lisa. Her eyes say it all. *She's staying.*

Alright. Be stupid.

Lisa heads downstairs. *The Mamas and Papas continue.*

Susanna sits there, listening to Lisa's ransacking downstairs. Then – *a door slams.* Daisy's body swings gently in the background. Ruby nuzzles against Susanna's leg. Susanna takes the cat, holding it – suddenly, she shudders.

A siren rises. A knock on the door downstairs.

MEDIC

Hello – *hello?*

SUSANNA

– *up here* –

A phasing organ rises. A drum pounds a funereal rhythm.
HIGH ANGLE DOWN ON: SUSANNA IN THE BATHROOM DOOR.

TWO MEDICS BARREL UP THE STAIRS.

CUT TO:

EXT. 23 REVERE STREET – DAY – RAIN

Rain pours down. The funereal drum continues.

DAISY'S COVERED BODY IS WHEELED INTO AN AMBULANCE.

MELVIN pulls up in a car. He emerges, ashen, as – THE
AMBULANCE PULLS AWAY INTO THE RAIN.

SUSANNA sits with RUBY, smoking beneath an awning.

CUT TO:

INT. MELVIN'S CAR – DRIVING BACK TO CLAYMOORE – RAIN – DAY

Ftsssk, ftsssk, ftsssk. The wipers churn.
SUSANNA leans against the glass. Deep in thought.
Rain drips past her face. Ruby against her chest. She is very
beautiful at the moment. MELVIN drives – grim. *We've never seen
him like this. Clearly shaken, lost in his world.*

Susanna turns, cocks her head. She looks at Melvin. He does not
meet her eyes. She continues to stare. He says nothing. *Ftsssk,
ftsssk go the wipers.* Susanna turns back to the moving world.

*On a main street, they pass shoppers scurrying to their cars. A mother
pushes her crying child into a station-wagon. Susanna speak quietly.*

                    SUSANNA
        Does every crazy person have a secret?

The question hangs there in the air. *Ftsssk, ftsssk.* After a beat,
Melvin replies, curt –

                    MELVIN
        – *What* are you talking about?

                    SUSANNA
                (undeterred, gentle)
        Like in the movies – like in *Marnie* – where she remembers
        her mom was a whore and murdered this sailor. Or in *Psycho*
        where he doesn't want anyone to know his mother is dead.
                (beat)
        – or like Daisy. *With her dad.*

Ftsssk, ftsssk – go the wipers.

                    MELVIN
        Sometimes, there is no secret.

123

SUSANNA

Then why do people go crazy?

A therapist without an answer to the question of his life:

MELVIN

I don't know.

SUSANNA

Maybe they're just broken – maybe their circuits are crossed
and they just want to blame someone. For their bad luck.

MELVIN

Maybe.

SUSANNA

Maybe happiness is just another commodity. Like pork bellies
or crude oil. Maybe there's only so much of it to go around.

MELVIN

Maybe.

SUSANNA

Maybe they think too much.

MELVIN

Maybe.

A car passes, throwing water up.

SUSANNA

You know. I see things and I look at things and I see patterns
and people. I stare at my hand and sometimes it has no bones
– but I don't know what it means. I move through it and
around it, I go backward and forward – but there's nothing.
There's no secret in my past. I didn't set myself on fire. I
wasn't molested. There were some sad people. Some
mistakes. But no big secrets. And if it all doesn't mean
anything, Melvin – if there's no big secret – then I'm just
losing time. All the time. I'm losing time. I'm broken. I'm a
zombie. I'm the saddest crazy of all. I've got no one to blame.
I'm a broken refrigerator. My thoughts are all misfires.
Someone should kick me.

> MELVIN

Someone just did.

Susanna thinks about this – wipes the tears from her eyes. Out the window, through the rain, CLAYMOORE APPROACHES. *Ftsssk, ftsssk go the wipers.*

> CUT TO:

INT. SOUTH BELL – LOBBY – LATE AFTERNOON

JANET, M-G, POLLY, GEORGINA and CYNTHIA in the TV ROOM. They fall silent as SUSANNA enters, holding RUBY. She walks past them, wordless. All eyes on her. MELVIN nods to MARGIE.

> MELVIN

Send someone for a litter box.

> CUT TO:

INT. SOUTH BELL – SUSANNA AND GEORGINA'S ROOM – SUNSET

SUSANNA lies on the bed. Ruby on her belly. GEORGINA enters.

> GEORGINA

Hey.

A clatter of scuffing shoes. M-G, JANET, POLLY and CYNTHIA awkwardly shuffle into the doorway. They all smile sweetly.

> POLLY

– Can I pet the kitty?

Susanna hands RUBY to POLLY, who takes it *very carefully.* All the others surround POLLY and RUBY, *cooing – jealous.*

> SUSANNA

Careful.

Susanna lies back. She closes her eyes.

> CUT TO:

INT. SUSANNA AND GEORGINA'S ROOM – NIGHT

Click, swish.

                              MARGIE
        Checks.

Susanna sits in bed writing. It is dark. Margie snaps on the
overhead light.

        You're gonna ruin your eyes.

Susanna looks at the caged bulb burning above her.

                                                    CUT TO:

INT. SOUTH BELL – HYDROTHERAPY ROOM – MORNING

SUSANNA sits in the bubbling tub.

VALERIE walks in with a razor, sits down.

                              SUSANNA
        Hey.

Valerie hands the razor to Susanna and looks away.

        Where's John?

                              VALERIE
        'moved – to men's.

Susanna nods sadly. Shaves her legs.

                                                    CUT TO:

INT. MELVIN'S OFFICE – DAY

MELVIN packs up his office. He looks awful. Dead. SUSANNA sits,
staring out the window, sadly.

                              SUSANNA
        You shouldn't have let her out.

                              MELVIN
        A year of analysis doesn't make you a shrink, Susanna.

                              SUSANNA
        And you shouldn't have let her keep chickens in her room.
        You wouldn't let *me* do that.

                                126

                            MELVIN
I didn't have a choice, Susanna. It's what her father wanted.
He was her guardian. He wanted her out.

                            SUSANNA
You're rationalizing, Melvin.

                            MELVIN
No – I'm quitting.

                            SUSANNA
It's a mistake. That's all.

                            MELVIN
Well. You're going to be very happy, then. Because Dr Wick
is brilliant. She never makes mistakes.

Susanna turns from the window. She stares at A TRINKET ON HIS
DESK. *It dawns on her.*

                            SUSANNA
    You asshole.

Melvin looks up. His eyes dead.

    You were screwing her, too.

Melvin says nothing. Numb. He goes back to packing.

    'Getting fucked by her dad and her shrink. No wonder she
    killed herself two ways.

Susanna walks out.

                                                    CUT TO:

INT. SOUTH BELL – OUTSIDE DAISY'S ROOM – DAY

Valerie stands slumped with a mop, smoking.

                            SUSANNA
You're not supposed to smoke on duty.

                            VALERIE
Report me.

                              127

SUSANNA sees that Valerie has tears in her eyes. As soon as their eyes meet, more tears come to Valerie.

> SUSANNA
> – Someone else can do that.

> VALERIE
> There's a new girl coming. I've cleaned this room six times in the last two weeks – and I still can't get the smell out.

Susanna smiles.

> I try not to get attached, but it's hard.

Valerie strokes Susanna's hair. Touches her cheek.

> I'm sorry about what I –

> SUSANNA
> I was the pig. You were right. I have to get down to business.

> VALERIE
> Baby. You just lived through something intense. What you got to do now is *take your time*.

Susanna looks up at Valerie. Intense.

> SUSANNA
> I'm out of time.

> CUT TO:

EXT. CLAYMOORE GROUNDS – AFTERNOON

SUSANNA walks the grounds with POLLY, JANET AND GRETTA. Polly joyfully walks RUBY on a leash.

Susanna sees JOHN, PULLING SUMMER PLANTINGS FROM A TRACTOR. Susanna crosses to him. He does not look up.

> SUSANNA
> John.

> JOHN
> I'm not supposed to talk to you.

> SUSANNA

Come on.

> JOHN

I don't feel like losing my job, alright?

> SUSANNA

Hey – I'm sorry – I'm really sorry.

> JOHN
> (he turns)

For what? *Kissing me?*

> SUSANNA

Yeah.

Disgusted, he turns back to his work.

– I mean – No –
I'm sorry you got in trouble for it.

> JOHN

It's okay. It wasn't gonna amount to much, was it? Just another crazy-rich-girl-game.

> SUSANNA

What are you talking about?

> JOHN

I coulda' gone to Harvard for how much it costs your dad to keep you here.
> (beat)
You people are different, that's all.

John climbs onto a tractor, starting it up. Susanna is stung. *In the background, Polly cackles with joy, playing with the cat.*

> CUT TO:

INT. SOUTH BELL – SUSANNA'S ROOM – NIGHT

Leaf-laced light plays on the ceiling. *No monster.*

SUSANNA in bed. Her face scrunched. Checks her hand.

RUBY lies on her belly, watching her. Curious. Susanna looks back to her journal, scribbling.

> SUSANNA
> (voice-over)
> Thought is a hard thing to control.

CUT TO:

INT. DINING ROOM – MORNING

SUSANNA eats her breakfast.

All the girls eat around her, but she speaks to no one.

> SUSANNA
> (voice-over)
> Many things we do – like breathing or
> digestion – require no thought at all.

CUT TO:

INT. ART THERAPY ROOM – DAY

THE OTHER GIRLS giggle and pass time as –

SUSANNA works on A FINGER PAINTING OF A GIANT TONGUE.

It is the mother of all tongues, humungous, radiating light, curvaceous and strong. The paint is thick and luminous.

> SUSANNA
> (voice-over)
> In fact, you can screw up your bodily
> functions by thinking about them.
> I'll give you an example –

CUT TO:

SUSANNA LIES FACE UP ON A LEATHER COUCH.

Susanna's voice-over becomes present dialogue. She continues speaking as she stares at the ceiling:

– you're about to stand up and put your dishes away after breakfast, right? But suddenly – you think about your *tongue*.

130

DR WICK sits in her leather chair, taking notes, listening. Red and orange leaves blow outside her window.

– and once you think about your tongue – suddenly it becomes this intrusion in your mouth. You think. Why's it so large? Why's it all scratchy on the sides?

Very subtly, Dr Wick plays with her tongue in her mouth.

Maybe you can remove it. There'd be more room. But what's really amazing is – just from thinking about it – your tongue has become enormous. All of a sudden, it's this fat swollen thing inside your mouth.

DR WICK

What do you do?

SUSANNA

You try to think it smaller

Wick smiles. *Good answer.*

DR WICK

How do you do that?

SUSANNA

I don't know. Maybe something happens. You hear a bird sing or the radio or something. And while your brain is somewhere else, your tongue gets smaller. But then – thinking of it getting smaller makes it *big again.*
                    (beat)
All this takes five minutes and all I ever wanted to do was scrape my dishes.

DR WICK

So, maybe it takes five minutes for you to scrape your dishes.

SUSANNA

It's not *efficient.*

DR WICK

Perhaps. But perhaps the essence of you is not efficient.

Susanna turns from the ceiling – looking for the first time at Dr Wick. She smiles in a way we've never seen.

> SUSANNA
>
> You think maybe I'm gifted? Maybe I have ESP or something and I'm actually the next stage of evolutionary development and no one gets it because they're stupid?

Wick smiles. *The grandfather clock chimes.*

> You think I can be home by Thanksgiving?

> DR WICK
>
> I'd be happy to give you a weekend pass –

> SUSANNA
>
> No. I want it real. If I get out – I want it real.
> (reminding her)
> Nothing's happened for weeks, you know.

> DR WICK
>
> Except your tongue.

> SUSANNA
>
> *Come on, Sonia.* Isn't the whole point that it's never going away.

> DR WICK
>
> The point is *control.*

> SUSANNA
>
> And here I am. In control. Off meds. No headaches. Sleeping sound. *Come on.*

A long beat. Susanna glares – dead serious.

> DR WICK
>
> I'll consider it.

TRANSITION TO:

INT. SOUTH BELL – TV ROOM – AFTERNOON

VALERIE AND SOME OF THE GIRLS take down PAPER TURKEYS. Cynthia and Janet rummage through a box of Christmas ornaments. GEORGINA sits – riveted in front of the television.

ON TV: THE WIZARD OF OZ. *The Wizard takes off in a hot air balloon, leaving Dorothy behind. Dorothy cries. Music surges.*

SUSANNA glances up from her journal to THE TELEVISION. *On the screen,* THE GREAT PINK BUBBLE *of Glinda the Good floats down upon Emerald city.*

> GLINDA THE GOOD
> – *You don't need to be helped any longer. You've always had the power to go back to Kansas.*

> SCARECROW
> *Then why didn't you tell her before?*

> GLINDA THE GOOD
> *She wouldn't have believed me. She had to learn it for herself.*

Susanna is amused – she looks to –

GEORGINA, tears drizzling. A peak moment.

SUSANNA LOOKS TO: VALERIE ON THE PHONE IN THE NURSES' STATION, concerned. She whispers something to Margie.

OUTSIDE: A POLICE CAR pulls around the building. Susanna meets eyes with Valerie as she crosses toward:

> CUT TO:

INT. SUSANNA AND GEORGINA'S ROOM

RUBY watches curiously as SUSANNA stares out of her window.

BELOW: A POLICE OFFICER OPENS THE BACK DOOR OF HIS CAR – EXTENDING HIS HAND TO HELP OUT *LISA*.

Oblivious, POLLY ENTERS SUSANNA'S ROOM, carrying THE UKULELE from the peg board. She plucks some notes.

> POLLY
> Look what Valerie gave me this morning.

Below: Lisa mouths a '*Fuck you, pig!*' to the cop. Her jeans are muddy. Her elegant hands cuffed behind her back. Her lip is cut. Her cheek bruised. *Strung out.*

                    SUSANNA
                    (distant)
I thought you weren't allowed to play with that.

                    POLLY
                (plucking like a minstrel)
Valerie said the strings are too short to hang myself and too
soft to cut myself and life's too short to say no to me every
'god damned day'.

Susanna smiles, tense, and turns, looking out the door at:

VALERIE AND OTHERS ON ALERT AS – LISA ENTERS WITH THE
COPS. Lisa is zombie-like, dead-eyed.

                POLICE OFFICER
'bought some bad PCP.

                    VALERIE
There's good PCP?

Valerie nods to AN ORDERLY, who take Lisa by the arms. She
defiantly puts her arms over her head in a POW style. As she's
escorted past Susanna's door, toward Seclusion:

LISA SMILES AT SUSANNA. Her face battered.

                                    CUT TO:

INT. SOUTH BELL – HALL OUTSIDE SECLUSION – MORNING

THROUGH THE MESHED GLASS: LISA SLEEPS on the bare mattress.

SUSANNA PEERS IN – LOOKING AT HER. She taps on the glass. But
Lisa does not move. *Susanna taps again.* Lisa stirs. She sees
Susanna through the door. Susanna smiles.

Lisa crosses to the door. She tries to open it – but it is locked. She
looks up, weary. *Her voice muffled through glass.*

                    LISA
What do you want?

                    SUSANNA
'just wanted to say hey. It's been a while.

                    134

Lisa nods. Softens. Looks down.

You okay?

> LISA
> They're gonna put me through the grinder for a few weeks.

Lisa looks up, meeting Susanna's eyes. She loops a finger through the steel mesh. Like a child. Tears well in her eyes.

Susanna smiles, pressing her finger against Lisa's through the glass. The moment is interrupted when *Valerie calls:*

> VALERIE
> Susanna. We're late.

Susanna turns. VALERIE stands in the lobby, waiting.

> SUSANNA
> (turning back)
> I have to go. Dr Wick.

> LISA
> They still fucking with you?

> SUSANNA
> I think they're – I mean, actually *I know* – they're letting me out.

The last three words hang heavy in the air. They are devastating to Lisa – but she smiles through it.

> LISA
> – oh – *great* –

CUT TO:

INT. DOCTORS' MEETING ROOM – LATE AFTERNOON

DR WICK and DR CORNISH sit behind a long table along with a hospital social worker, MISS PLIMACK.

SUSANNA is seated in front of them. Beside VALERIE.

> DR WICK
> Susanna, you become an *outpatient* in a couple days – and it's essential there be a safety net in place.

Susanna nods.

This is Miss Plimack, your social worker.

SUSANNA

Hi.

MISS PLIMACK

Hello, Susanna. Can you fill me in on any arrangements you've made?

SUSANNA

They haven't told you anything?

DR WICK

Susanna.

MISS PLIMACK

I want to hear it *from you.*

SUSANNA

My dad got me a part-time job – at a book store in Harvard Square. I got an apartment there and a phone – so I can – you know –

MISS PLIMACK

– stay in touch –

SUSANNA

And I'm gonna see Sonia twice a week.

MISS PLIMACK

So, is that your long-term plan – to work in retail?

SUSANNA

My plan? No.

MISS PLIMACK

Then what do you plan to do?

SUSANNA

I plan to write. A lot.

Susanna looks about, waiting for someone to laugh.

MISS PLIMACK

Are you travelling directly to Cambridge?

SUSANNA

Um. No – I'm spending the weekend with my parents.

MISS PLIMACK

How are you getting there?

SUSANNA

Hovercraft.

Cornish and Plimack look to Dr Wick.

DR WICK

Don't be cavalier, Susanna. I can reverse this decision. Things
will happen out there. Jarring things. Things that test your
resolve. If you consider this journey over – you're mistaken.

CUT TO:

INT. SOUTH BELL – TV ROOM – NIGHT

JANET AND SUSANNA look out through the frost on the windows.
In the background, *McWilley hands out meds, calling names* . . .

JANET

Maybe you'll have a white Christmas.

MCWILLEY

. . . Susanna Kaysen . . .

McWilley holds out a white cup containing TWO GREEN PILLS.

SUSANNA

What are these?

MCWILLEY

Sleeping pills, darling. You want to be rested tomorrow,
don't you? *'Last night is always a long one.*

Tempted to argue, Susanna throws back the pills like a pro. She
turns and walks away – spitting them into her palm, pocketing
them, as she notices:

DOWN THE HALL: M-G SQUATS AT LISA'S DOOR (Seclusion). She scribbles in crayon, passing a note under the door. In seconds, the paper comes back – *and M-G reads it, cackling wildly, frighteningly, like a chimp.*

CUT TO:

INT. SUSANNA AND GEORGINA'S ROOM – LATER THAT NIGHT

GEORGINA sleeps peacefully.

RUBY sleeps, curled up on Susanna's Samsonite case.

SUSANNA lies in bed, wide awake. *Suddenly there is a blood curdling scream down the hall. A woman's voice, crying out hysterically.*

Susanna lies in bed, frozen, wide-eyed. She looks to – Georgina – fast asleep. *The off-screen screaming continues and we hear Mrs McWilley's voice barking orders to HECTOR AND AN ORDERLY.* SUSANNA CROSSES TO THE DOOR.

IN THE DARKENED HALL

M-G – HYSTERICAL – IN A STRAIT-JACKET – IS DRAGGED OUT THE MAIN DOOR BY MCWILLEY AND AN ORDERLY. The metal door slams – and the lobby is suddenly empty. *Quiet. Moonlit.*

Susanna looks down the hall toward:

THE SECLUSION ROOM: a glow of green light in its window.

SUSANNA TURNS, HEADS QUICKLY BACK INTO – HER ROOM.

She jumps back on to her bed, reaching in the vents of her heater, producing THE TWO GREEN SLEEPING PILLS. She swallows them and lies back, staring upward.

The wind rattles against the glass. The pull cord to the shades swings from the draft, tapping on the glass. *Tap, tap, tappa, tap, tap.*

Leaf-laced moonlight plays and swirls on the ceiling. The shadows form a vague face. A man's face? *We have seen this before in Susanna's bedroom.*

Susanna's eyes flutter with the onset of the drug.

SUSANNA

No.

She closes her eyes. From somewhere distant – *a meow*.

Susanna's eyes open. She looks to –

HER SAMSONITE CASE – *RUBY IS GONE.*

Ruby?

Susanna turns – *GEORGINA IS GONE.*

CUT TO:

INT. SOUTH BELL – HALLWAY – NIGHT

Susanna moves down the hall toward:

THE GREEN LIGHT OF THE SECLUSION ROOM DOOR.

She stops, checks in the door of Polly's room.

SUSANNA

Polly?

Polly is gone. Just the Catatonic sleeping.

She walks on – closer, closer to – the seclusion room. The door is cracked open – Susanna pushes it further. *It creaks.* She peers in.

Empty. Just the scratched walls.

But from somewhere – *meeeooow*.
Susanna moves on down the hall. Her heart racing.

CUT TO:

INT. SOUTH BELL – TV ROOM/HALL

Susanna pads quietly past the flickering TV. She spins around at the slightest sound. *Meoow*.

SUSANNA

Ruby.

INT. ART ROOM – NIGHT

The meows emanate from THE FIRE STAIRS. A WIND BLOWS. THE
DOOR IS OPEN – leading downward. Susanna backs up,
hyperventilating.

> SUSANNA
> Stop it! *STOP IT!*

> LISA
> (off-screen; from downstairs)
> A sweet boy kisses you at a party. You can a) kiss him back
> knowing he'll want you forever, or b) push him away, hurting
> a sweet boy.

Susanna enters the staircase.

CUT TO:

INT. STAIRS/TUNNELS – NIGHT

Susanna climbs down the stairs.

> SUSANNA
> No, no, no . . .

She moves instinctively down the wet dark corridor toward the
reverberating sound of Lisa's voice.

> LISA
> (off-screen)
> A college guy kisses you at a party. You can a) kiss him back
> knowing it means nothing to him, or b) push him away,
> knowing it means nothing to him.

Creosote drips from the walls making Rorschach-like designs.

> Your *father's friend* kisses you at a party. Now *this* is special.

*There is a burst of girlish laughter: Polly, Georgina. Then the sound –
unmistakable – of Lisa,* silencing them.

> *SHUT UP!*

(reading)
. . . That's the best of all because you can *both* kiss him back knowing it means everything, *and* push him away because he won't blow his life!

Susanna spins in circles, looking about in the blackness. She knocks over some empty cans - THEY CLATTER LOUDLY.

SUSANNA
LISA – WHERE ARE YOU?!

Light moves down a tunnel. Susanna chases it.

A CIGARETTE GLOWS ORANGE – LIGHTING LISA'S FACE.

LISA
Right here, baby. Why – *are you scared? Are we pushing your buttons?*

Lisa flicks on a flashlight, illuminating – SUSANNA'S JOURNAL.

TWO OTHER FLASHLIGHTS CLICK ON.

POLLY AND GEORGINA stand behind Lisa. Polly holds RUBY.

POLLY
Hey, Susanna.

LISA
(smiles)
We're reading your book. Since it's your last night, we thought we'd have a little *salon* – celebrate all the wisdom you're carrying into the world. Maybe learn a few things to help us grow as people.

SUSANNA
(calmly)
That is mine. Lisa. *That* is *mine.*

LISA
We learned how – when you were baby, they strapped you to a board. And how you think Georgina doesn't really want to leave – and Polly never will – and how I'm criminally insane.

141

LISA FLIPS TO THE BACK OF THE JOURNAL, reading by flashlight, she walks in circles around Susanna:

'Lisa's eyes – once so magnetic – now just look empty.'

SUSANNA
(turning to Georgina)
Georgina, what are you doing down here?

LISA
'Georgina lies only to the people who keep her here. Maybe she wants to live in Oz forever.' *Ooooo. How perceptive!*

Georgina turns toward Susanna, dead-eyed.

GEORGINA
You better erase that thing about me. My father is the head of the CIA and he could have you dead in *minutes*.

LISA
(flipping more pages)
'In this world, looks are everything. Sometimes I think Polly's sweetness is just a desperate attempt to make it easier for us to look at her.'

SUSANNA LOOKS TO POLLY – WHO IS STRICKEN, HURT.

LISA COMES TO A STOP, BLOCKING THE WAY SUSANNA CAME.

So nice of you to pass judgement on us. Now that you're cured.

THE LIGHT SHINES PIERCINGLY AT SUSANNA. She backs down a tunnel as Lisa advances.

You know, the sex scenes get a bit *redundant*. The Professor groping you – the English teacher in his Karman Ghia – and Toby, your little draftee. *All grabbing.* Clutching. *Hands – hands – hands all over –*

SUSANNA
What the *fuck* are you doing?

Lisa snaps the flashlight back on herself.

LISA

Playing the villain, baby. It's what you wanted, isn't it? I try to give you everything you want.

SUSANNA

No, you don't.

LISA

You wanted your file. *I got your file.* You wanted out. *I got you out.* You needed money. *I found you some.* Needed a place to sleep. *I got you one.* I always told you the truth. *You liked that.* I'm fucking *consistent.* I didn't scribble it down in my secret book – I TOLD you the TRUTH. And I told Daisy the truth, too – what everyone knew but would not say – and *she killed herself.* I played the fucking villain. Just like you wanted.

SUSANNA

Why would I want that, Lisa?

LISA

Because it makes you the *good guy*, sweet pea! You come back here – sweetness and light, sad and contrite – and everyone sits, wringing their hands, congratulating you on all your *bravery.* Meanwhile, I'm blowing three guys in a bus station for the money that was *IN HER FUCKING ROBE!*

SUSANNA NOTICES A HYPODERMIC STUFFED IN LISA'S POCKET. SUSANNA BOLTS INTO A LOW SIDE TUNNEL.

POLLY

Stop! She's too scared, Lisa.

Fifty feet away, Polly stands crying in the tunnel.

LISA	POLLY
SHUT UP, POLLY!	Stop it, please . . .

CUT TO:

INT. LOW TUNNEL TO FURNACE ROOM

Lisa advances into the empty low tunnel. She walks toward the furnace room. Lighting another cigarette, singing to herself:

LISA

Oh, Susie Q. Oh, Susie Q, baby, I love you, Susie Q.

Georgina and Polly follow, holding the cat.
LISA PULLS OUT THE HYPODERMIC.

CUT TO:

INT. FURNACE ROOM – NIGHT

The flames of the furnace lick orange.
SUSANNA paces about, looking for another exit.
FOOTSTEPS: SUSANNA TURNS – SEES:

LISA APPROACHING. SHE TRIES TO SHUT THE DOOR, ONE HAND
ON THE KNOB, ONE IN THE JAM, TRYING TO GET IT UNSTUCK.
SUDDENLY IT BREAKS LOOSE, SMASHING *SUSANNA'S HAND!*
SUSANNA SCREAMS – PULLS BACK, staring at:

HER HAND: BLOODY, LIMP, FINGERS BROKEN. *It looks just like her
visions.*

SUSANNA

NO! *NO, NO, NO! STOP IT!*

LISA APPEARS IN THE CRACKED DOOR.

LISA

You talk dark, Susie Borderline. But you are a fake – You
can't even kill yourself right. Aspirin – it's like trying to
overdose on *Chiclets.*

Lisa pushes open the door, advancing on Susanna.

You know what? There's too many buttons in the world. All
begging to be pressed. All just BEGGING to be PRESSED!

Lisa hears Georgina and Polly down the hall. Tears fill Lisa's eyes
as she looks up and about.

And it makes me wonder. *Why* the *fuck doesn't anyone ever
press mine!? Why doesn't anyone press my buttons? Why am I so
neglected?*

Susanna holds her wounded hand, walking backward.

Why doesn't anyone ever tell me I'm *a fucking whore? Why doesn't anyone tell me how happy my family would be – if I were dead?!*

SUSANNA

Because you're dead already.

Lisa stops in her tracks.

All this time – I've been wondering what this thing *is*, this black thing, whipping me around. This thing in my head, in my hand, in my bed, on my wall – I've indulged it, I've kissed it, I've fucked it – but I've never seen its face – *until now –*

Lisa stands there – stunned by Susanna's words. No one's ever talked to her this way.

POLLY AND GEORGINA STAND IN THE DOOR.

No one cares if you die, because you're *dead already. You're the walking dead. That's your real button, Lisa. That's why you keep coming back. You need this place – to feel alive. It's pathetic.*

A HOWL OF WIND. THE TRANSOM WINDOW RATTLES.

I've wasted *a YEAR of my LIFE.*
Maybe I'll see purple people and –
Maybe everyone out there is a mediocrity –
Maybe the whole world is STUPID AND
IGNORANT – BUT I'D RATHER BE *IN IT.*
I'D RATHER BE FUCKING IN IT
THAN DOWN HERE WITH *YOU*!

Weeping like a baby, LISA TURNS AWAY – TRIES TO JAM THE HYPODERMIC INTO HERSELF.

BUT SUSANNA TAKES IT AWAY, TOSSING IT INTO A PUDDLE. She rolls Lisa over. Lisa's eyes are red with anguish.

LISA

I am – I'm dead – *I'm dead –*

Lisa cries and cries like a child. She rolls into Susanna's lap. Susanna strokes her hair.

CLIMBING TO A CRACK BEHIND THE FURNACE – POLLY WATCHES, also weeping. She holds Ruby tightly.

GEORGINA drops light bulbs on the floor, singing to herself.

OUT THE MESHED TRANSOM – *DAWN LIGHT OVER THE CAMPUS.*

CUT TO:

INT. SOUTH BELL – HALLWAY – NEW DAY

CLOSE ON: A HAND, GRIPPING A SMALL GLASS OBJECT.

TILT UP TO: JANET, skittering down the hallway, avoiding nurses. She rounds a corner and bursts through a door –

INT. SOUTH BELL – BATHROOM – DAY

SUSANNA, her arm in a sling, looking weary, puts on make-up. She's wearing one of the dresses her mother had packed.

SUSANNA
Did you get it?

JANET NODS SOLEMNLY – HANDS SUSANNA THE GLASS OBJECT.

JANET
I had to trade with a transvestite in the men's ward – for *Soul on Ice.*

CUT TO:

INT. HALLWAY IN MAXIMUM SECURITY WARD – DAY

DR WICK AND DOCTOR CORNISH emerge from a room through AN INFIRMARY DOOR. Grim. Wick looks to –

SUSANNA waiting with VALERIE, smiles sadly.

DR WICK
You're alright?

Susanna nods, certain. Dr Wick nods and moves off. She looks back, adding:

She's not speaking.

146

Susanna looks to THE INFIRMARY DOOR.

VALERIE

You squeak – I'll be in there.

CUT TO:

INT. INFIRMARY ROOM – MAXIMUM SECURITY WARD – DAY

Susanna enters, approaching LISA, who lies in a bed by a narrow window. She's heavily medicated. Susanna sits on a stool beside the bed. They both just sit there. Lisa's eyes lift, meet Susanna's.

LISA

They cut my nails.

SUSANNA

But your hands are still beautiful.

Lisa looks down at HER LONG, TAPERING FINGERS. She tucks them in, hiding her short nails.

Here. *Give me your hand. Lisa.*

Lisa does as she's told. Susanna pulls out A BOTTLE OF RED NAIL POLISH [*what she got from Janet*]. She starts to paint what's left of Lisa's nails.

LISA LOOKS UP TO SUSANNA – TEARS IN HER EYES. She is very frightened. She speaks quietly.

LISA

I'm not really dead.

SUSANNA

I know.

Susanna continues painting her nails. *Lisa begins to weep.*

LISA

I'm gonna miss you.

SUSANNA

No. You're going to *get out of here* – and come and see me.

Lisa nods obediently. She touches Susanna's hand.

147

INT. SOUTH BELL NURSES' STATION – DAY

AT THE DOOR: VALERIE WAITS WITH SUSANNA'S BAG AS –

SUSANNA HUGS THE GIRLS GOODBYE – M-G, JANET, CYNTHIA.
GEORGINA stands back, looking down, avoiding Susanna's eyes.

> SUSANNA
> Hey. Georgina. What I write in my journal. I don't know
> what I'm saying. It's just thoughts. Maybe *I'm* the liar.

> GEORGINA
> Maybe not.

POLLY STANDS AT THE DOOR, TREMBLING – HOLDING RUBY OUT
FOR SUSANNA. *It's painful. She has fallen in love with the cat.*

Susanna crosses and is about to take the cat from her –

> SUSANNA
> If I leave Ruby here – will you take care of her for me? 'Let
> me play with her when I come for therapy? Polly?

Polly nods rapidly – ferociously. *Blubbers a laugh of joy. Holds the
cat to her chest.*

CUT TO:

EXT. CLAYMOORE – MORNING

SUSANNA walks from the hospital with VALERIE. She carries
nothing but her SAMSONITE BAG.

> VALERIE
> *I guess I better get more kitty litter.*

They cross through the light snow toward A BOSTON CAB IDLING
IN THE COLD AIR. Susanna sees JOHN, PULLING SACKS FROM A
TRACTOR. HE LOOKS UP.

> SUSANNA
> Um. Whatever's playing at the Brattle at eight on Tuesday –
> I'm gonna be there.

– *okay.*

He goes back to his work, watching her with a smile.

SUSANNA
(to Valerie)
Is he allowed to see an outpatient?

VALERIE
Honey. I can't control what goes on in that *ward.* I let the world be.

Susanna smiles – tosses in her case. She looks at Valerie –

Valerie takes her into her arms, tightly:

Think of me when you shave your legs.

Susanna laughs. Valerie steps back.

Susanna gets in the cab. Closes the door. It starts up, lurches forward.

Susanna lights a cigarette. Her eyes riveted on Valerie. *Valerie becomes a speck.*

Susanna looks toward SOUTH BELL AS THE CAB PASSES:

MOVING IN ON: GEORGINA – LOOKING OUT OF THE ART ROOM WINDOW.

SUSANNA
(voice-over)
If I'd been a liar, like Georgina,
you'd wonder how much I told you is true.

MOVING IN ON: LISA – LOOKING OUT OF HER WINDOW.

If I'd been a sociopath, like Lisa,
you'd wonder if I ever recovered.
Though she did make a life for herself.

MOVING IN ON: POLLY, JANET AND M-G IN THE HALL.

Pressed against the window, watching Susanna's cab move off.

Polly. I still have dreams about Polly.

FROM THE WINDOWS OF THE HOSPITAL. MOVING IN ON:

DR WICK WATCHES *as the cab drives away.*

My final diagnosis.
A recovered borderline.

Susanna's car turns onto the main road.

BACK TO: SUSANNA IN THE CAB.

What *that* means I still don't know.
Words taint everything.

Susanna turns, noticing THE DRIVER'S ID CARD on the dash. His name: MONTY HOOVER. She looks at:

MONTY. HIS EYES MEET HERS IN THE REAR-VIEW. He smiles.

MONTY

Hey.

SUSANNA

Hey.

MONTY

'Where we going?

SUSANNA

Seventeen Burlingame.

MONTY

Alright.

Monty nods, turns the wheel.

Susanna smiles to herself, amused.
She looks out of the window. We watch her from outside.

CLOUDS AND TREES MOVE IN REFLECTION UPON THE GLASS.
A gentle guitar sound rises.

SUSANNA
(voice-over)
Now. When something weird happens.

I ask myself, *Shit. Am I still crazy?*
I ask myself, *Was I crazy then?*
Or was I like that girl – in the painting.
Interrupted at the music of being nineteen.

Susanna turns. She looks at us through the glass. She looks
straight at us. Her eyes. Big. Brown. Alive. *Just like in the painting.*
She sees us.

BLACKNESS

CREDITS

SUSANNA KAYSEN	Winona Ryder
LISA	Angelina Jolie
NURSE VALERIE	Whoopi Goldberg
DR WICK	Vanessa Redgrave
POLLY	Elizabeth Moss
GEORGINA	Clea DuVall
DAISY	Brittany Murphy
TOBIAS JACOBS	Jared Leto
MELVIN	Jeffrey Tambor
JOHN	Travis Fine
CYNTHIA	Jillian Armenante

Written by	James Mangold
	Lisa Loomer
	Anna Hamilton Phelan
Based in the book by	Susanna Kaysen
Directed by	James Mangold
Produced by	Douglas Wick
	Cathy Konrad
	Winona Ryder
	Carol Bodie
Cinematography	Jack Green

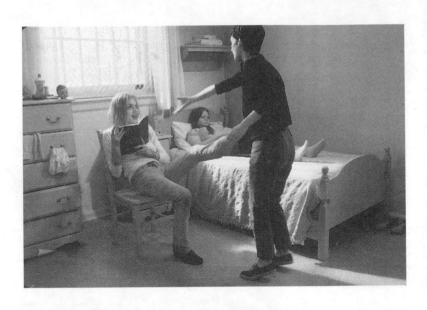

STORYBOARDS

Drawn by Alex Rubin

SC.1

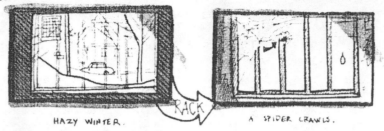

HAZY WINTER.

A SPIDER CRAWLS.

WATER DRIPS.

BLOOD.

FLAMES FLICKER...

ON A NEEDLE.

MEOW...

Opening sequence

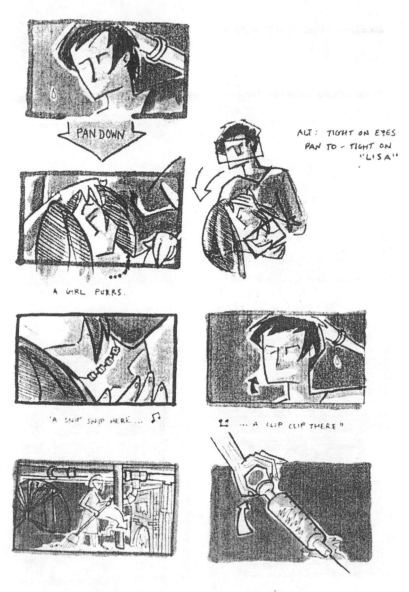

PAN DOWN

ALT: TIGHT ON EYES
PAN TO - TIGHT ON
"LISA"

A GIRL PURRS.

'A SNIP SNIP HERE... ♪

♫ ... A CLIP CLIP THERE"

"HERE THEY COME..."

FOOTSTEPS ECHO.

PAN DOWN

"PEOPLE ASK HOW WE GOT
IN THERE. WHAT THEY
REALLY WANT TO KNOW IS
IF THEY'RE LIKELY TO END
UP THERE AS WELL."

MEOW.

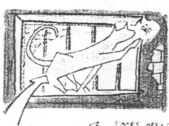

TILT
UP

SC 2

DOORS OPEN!

"ALL I CAN TELL YOU IS ... IT'S EASY."

SC.2 ER ROOM —

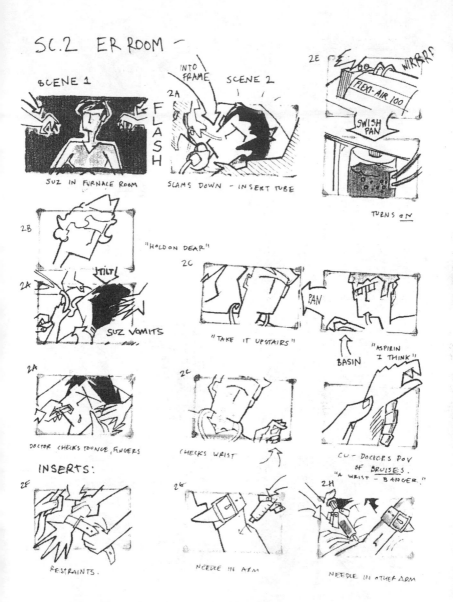

SCENE 1

SUZ IN FURNACE ROOM

FLASH

INTO FRAME   SCENE 2
2A

SLAMS DOWN — INSERT TUBE

2E   WIRRRR
FLEXI-AIR 100
SWISH PAN

TURNS ON

2B

"HOLD ON DEAR"

2A   TILT

SUZ VOMITS

2C

"TAKE IT UPSTAIRS"

PAN

BASIN

"ASPIRIN I THINK"

2A

DOCTOR CHECKS TOUNGE, FINGERS

2C

CHECKS WRIST

CU- DOCTORS POV
OF BRUISES.
"A WRIST — BANGER."

INSERTS:

2F

RESTRAINTS.

2G

NEEDLE IN ARM

2H

NEEDLE IN OTHER ARM

161

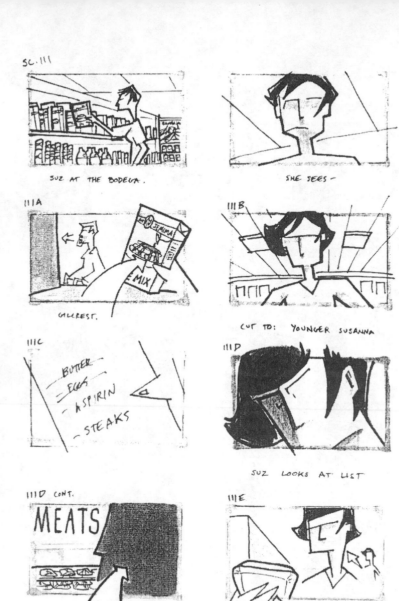

SC. 111

SUZ AT THE BODEGA.

SHE SEES —

111A

GILCREST.

111B

CUT TO: YOUNGER SUSANNA

111C

BUTTER
EGGS
ASPIRIN
STEAKS

111D

SUZ LOOKS AT LIST

111D CONT.

MEATS

RACK FOCUS. SHE LOOKS UP.

111E

SHE WALKS TOWARS US
AND CHOOSES —

Supermarket flashback

111F

2 STEAKS.

111G

111F

111G -ELU

111 I

BLOOD FILLS
THE CELLOPHANE...

111 H

THE BIN FILLS WITH BLOOD

(POSS. PAN
TO FEET)

111G

SHE LOOKS AT —

163

111J

111K

111L

BLOOD SPREADS - SUZ TURNS

111M

" SUSANNA ? "

111N

111O

BANANAS
29¢ LB

" CAN I HELP YOU DEAR ? "

The death of Daisy

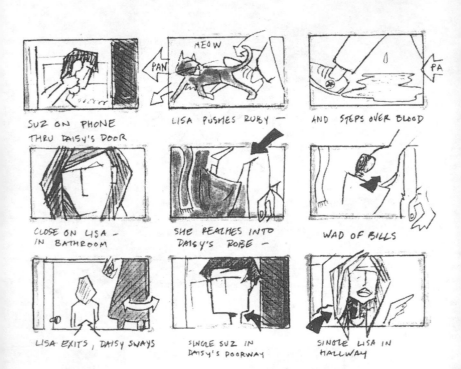

SUZ ON PHONE
THRU DAISY'S DOOR

LISA PUSHES RUBY —

AND STEPS OVER BLOOD

CLOSE ON LISA –
IN BATHROOM

SHE REACHES INTO
DAISY'S ROBE –

WAD OF BILLS

LISA EXITS, DAISY SWAYS

SINGLE SUZ IN
DAISY'S DOORWAY

SINGLE LISA IN
HALLWAY

SUZ SINKS DOWN
TO THE FLOOR

WIDE (TILT FROM SUZ?)
DAISY DEAD AGAINST WINDOW

166

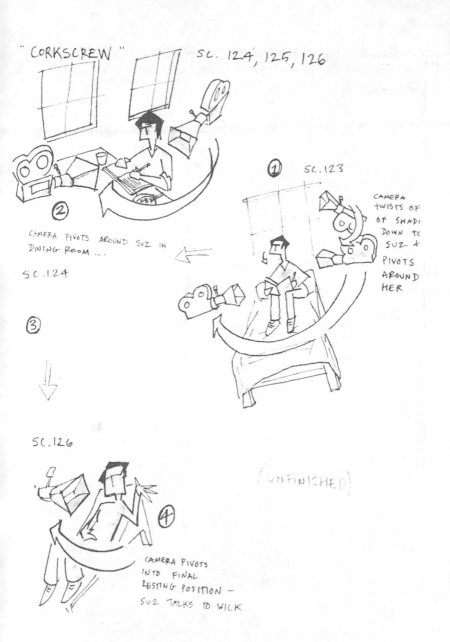

"CORKSCREW"   SC. 124, 125, 126

① SC.123

CAMERA TWISTS OFF OF SHADE DOWN TO SUZ & PIVOTS AROUND HER

② CAMERA PIVOTS AROUND SUZ IN DINING ROOM...

SC.124

③

SC.126

(UNFINISHED)

④ CAMERA PIVOTS INTO FINAL RESTING POSITION — SUZ TALKS TO WICK

Corkscrew camera moves around Susanna

'Not since Sylvia Plath's *The Bell Jar* has a personal account of life in a mental hospital achieved as much popularity and acclaim' – *Time Magazine*

In 1967, after a session with a psychiatrist she'd never seen before, eighteen-year-old Susanna Kaysen was put in a taxi and sent to McLean Hospital to be treated for depression. She spent most of the next two years on the ward for teenage girls in a psychiatric hospital renowned for its famous clientele – Sylvia Plath, Robert Lowell, James Taylor and Ray Charles.

A clear-sighted, unflinching work that provokes questions about our definitions of sane and insane, Kaysen's extraordinary memoir encompasses horror and razor-edged perception while providing vivid portraits of her fellow patients and their keepers.

Girl, Interrupted by Susanna Kaysen
is available in the UK from Virago at £5.99 (ISBN 1 86049 792 6)
and in the US from Vintage at $12.00 (ISBN 0 679 74604 8)

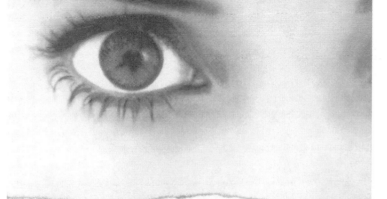

NATIONAL BESTSELLER
NOW A MAJOR MOTION PICTURE FROM COLUMBIA PICTURES
STARRING WINONA RYDER AND ANGELINA JOLIE

GIRL, INTERRUPTED

SUSANNA KAYSEN

"Poignant, honest and triumphantly
funny . . . [a] compelling and
heartbreaking story." —Susan Cheever,
The New York Times Book Review